PLASTIC CANVAS

Celebration Gifts

The Needlecraft Shop

PUBLISHER / Donna Robertson
EDITORIAL DIRECTOR / Carolyn Brooks Christmas
DESIGN DIRECTOR / Fran Rohus
CREATIVE DIRECTOR / Greg Smith
PRODUCTION DIRECTOR / Ange Workman

EDITORIAL

Editor / Janet Tipton
Composing Editors / Susan Koellner, Joni Sheedy, Jennifer Simcik
Associate Editors / Kristine Hart, Sharon Lothrop, Pauline Rosenberger, Cynthia Stodola
Proofreaders / Nancy Clevenger, Mary Lingle
Editorial Assistants / Janice Kellenberger, Jessica Rice
Publisher's Assistant / Marianne Telesca
Graphics / Derek Gentry, Debby Keel, Pauline Rosenberger

PHOTOGRAPHY

Art Directors / Rusty Lingle, Diane Simpson, Minette Collins Smith
Photographers / Renée Agee, Mary Craft, Tammy Cromer-Campbell
Cover Photo / Mary Craft

PRODUCTION

Assistant Production Director / Betty Gibbs Radla
Technical Director / Production / John J. Nosal

BOOK DESIGN

Art and Production / Sullivan Rothe Design

PRODUCT DESIGN

Design Coordinator / Brenda Wendling

BUSINESS

President / Jerry Gentry
Vice President / Customer Service / Karen Pierce
Vice President / Marketing / Greg Deily
Vice President / M.I.S. / John Trotter

CREDITS

Sincerest thanks to all the designers, manufacturers and other professionals whose dedication has made this book possible. Special thanks to Karla Peterson of Spectrum Color Center of Golden, CO, and Lori Powers, R.R. Donnelley & Sons Company, Chicago, IL.

Library of Congress Cataloging-in-Publication Data

ISBN: 0-9638031-2-3
First Printing: 1994
Library of Congress Catalogue Number: 93-86079
Published and Distributed by *The Needlecraft Shop, Inc.*
Printed in the United States of America.

ACKNOWLEDGMENTS

We would like to express our appreciation to the many people who helped create this book. Our special thanks go to each of the talented designers who contributed original designs.

Thanks, also, to all the talented and skilled editors, art directors, photographers and production staff whose technical expertise made this book come together.

In addition, we would like to thank the companies and individuals who provided locations for photography, models, props or other contributions.

Finally we wish to express our gratitude to the following manufacturers for their generous contribution of materials and supplies:

ALEENE'S™
+ Thick Designer Tacky Glue — My Little Wagon

ANCHOR®
+ Pearl cotton — Baby's Here!

MPR ASSOCIATES
+ Creative Twist™ twisted paper ribbon — Birdhouse Wreath, Colorful Corn

LOCTITE CORPORATION®
+ Silicone Gel by Creatively Yours® — Heart Brush

DARICE®
+ Nylon Plus™ yarn — Dress Up, Party Favors, My Little Wagon, Cottontail Parade, Birdhouse Wreath, Pastel Baskets, Sweetheart Keepsakes, Gift Wrap Box, Cardinal Wreath, Bountiful Harvest, Mallards & Cattails, Apple Checkers, Orchid Angles
+ Metallic cord — Sweetheart Keepsakes, Winter Sparkle
+ Ultra Stiff™ canvas — Birthday Cake Box
+ 5-count canvas — Watermelon Picnic
+ Designer canvas — Decorative Brooms
+ Colored canvas — Winter Sparkle
+ Crafty Circles™ — Winter Sparkle
+ Plastic canvas circles — Birthday Cake Box, Carriage Ride

+ Bird — Birdhouse Wreath
+ Grapevine wreath — Birdhouse Wreath
+ Mirror — Dress Up

DMC
+ Pearl cotton — Pastel Baskets
+ Embroidery floss — Gobbler Tissue Cover

KREINIK
+ Metallic braid — Independence Day

SPINRITE®
+ Plastic canvas yarn — Heart Brush

UNIEK® CRAFTS
+ Needloft™ yarn — Basket Buddies, Pastel Baskets, Independence Day, Carriage Ride, Gobbler Tissue Cover, Decorative Brooms, Corn Wreath, Winter Sparkle, Angelic Herald, Victorian Sleigh, Heart Fridgies, Heart Plant Poke, Heart Tissue Cover, Dainty Gift Bag, Iris Box, Card Party
+ Quick Count™ canvas — Independence Day
+ Quick Count™ Artist Size® canvas — Decorative Brooms
+ Metallic cord — Angelic Herald

Dear Friend,

From simple spur-of-the-moment gifts for friends to elaborately planned special-occasion gifts, every treasure you give is more meaningful when it's handmade.

The versatile techniques and stitches of plastic canvas needlepoint offer endless opportunities to create beautiful, easy-to-make projects that are perfect for gift giving. Every occasion will be a celebration accented with gifts you have lovingly created, stitch by stitch.

Each project in this collection is as much fun to make as it is to give – in fact, you'll want to select a few designs to create just for yourself! As you turn these pages, you'll discover a stunning display of imaginative ideas ready to help you plan every gift-giving occasion of the year.

Some items are quick and easy, suitable for completing at the last minute. Others are more detailed, sure to give you hours of stitching enjoyment as you create a treasure that will be proudly displayed for years to come.

Carolyn

CONTENTS

Basic Instructions to Get You Started

Most plastic canvas stitchers love getting their projects organized before they even step out the door in search of supplies. A few moments of careful planning can make the creation of your project even more fun.

First of all, prepare your work area. You will need a flat surface for cutting and assembly, and you will need a place to store your materials. Good lighting is essential, and a comfortable chair will make your stitching time even more enjoyable.

Do you plan to make one project, or will you be making several of the same item? A materials list appears at the beginning of each pattern. If you plan to make several of the same item, multiply your materials accordingly.

Canvas

Most projects can be made using standard-size sheets of canvas. Standard-size sheets of 7-count (7 holes per inch) are 70 x 90 holes and are about 10½"x 13½". For larger projects, 7-count canvas also comes in 12" x 18" (80 x 120 holes) and 13½" x 22½" (90 x 150 holes) sheets. Other shapes are available in 7-count, including circles, diamonds, ovals and purse forms.

10-count canvas (10 holes per inch) comes only in standard-size sheets, which vary slightly depending on brand. They are 10½" x 13½" (106 x 136 holes) or 11" x 14" (108 x 138 holes).

Newer canvas like 5-count (5 holes per inch) and 14-count (14 holes per inch) are also becoming popular with plastic canvas designers.

Some canvas is soft and pliable, while other canvas is stiffer and more rigid. To prevent canvas from cracking during or after stitching, you'll want to choose pliable canvas for projects that require shaping, like round baskets with curved handles. If your project is a box or an item that will stand alone, stiffer canvas is more suitable.

Both 7- and 10-count canvas are available in a rainbow of colors. Most designs can be stitched on colored as well as clear canvas. When a pattern does not specify color in the materials list, you can assume clear canvas was used in the photographed model. If you'd like to stitch only a portion of the design, leaving a portion unstitched, use colored canvas to coordinate with yarn colors.

Buy the same brand of canvas for each entire project. Different brands of canvas may differ slightly in the distance between each bar.

Supplies

Yarn, canvas, needles, cutters and most other supplies needed to complete the projects in this book are available through craft and needlework stores and mail order catalogs. Other supplies are available at fabric, hardware and discount stores. For mail order information, see page 160.

Marking & Counting Tools

To avoid wasting canvas, careful cutting of each piece is important. For some pieces with square corners, you might be comfortable cutting the canvas without marking it beforehand. But for pieces with lots of angles and cutouts, you may want to mark your canvas before cutting.

To count holes on the graphs, look for the bolder lines showing each ten holes. These ten-count lines begin in the lower left-hand corner of each graph and are on the graph to make counting easier. To count holes on the canvas, you may use your tapestry needle, a toothpick or a plastic hair roller pick. Insert the needle or pick slightly in each hole as you count.

Most stitchers have tried a variety of marking tools and have settled on a favorite, which may be crayon, permanent marker or grease pencil. One of the best marking tools is a fine-point overhead projection marker, available at office supply stores. The ink is dark and easy to see and washes off completely with water. After cutting and before stitching, it's important to remove all marks so they won't stain yarn as you stitch or show through stitches later. Cloth and paper toweling remove grease pencil and crayon marks, as do used fabric softener sheets.

Needles & Other Stitching Tools

Blunt-end tapestry needles are used for stitching plastic canvas. Choose a No. 16 needle for stitching 7-count and a No. 18 for stitching 10-count. Keep a small pair of embroidery scissors handy for snipping yarn. Try using needle-nose jewelry pliers for pulling the needle through several thicknesses of canvas and out of tight spots too small for your hand.

Cutting Tools

You may find it helpful to have several tools on hand for cutting canvas. When cutting long, straight sections, scissors, craft cutters or kitchen shears are the fastest and easiest to use. For cutting out detailed areas and trimming nubs, you may like using manicure scissors or nail clippers. If you prefer laying your canvas flat when cutting, try a craft knife and cutting surface — self-healing mats designed for sewing, as well as kitchen cutting boards, work well.

Yarn and Other Stitching Materials

You may choose two-ply nylon plastic canvas yarn (the color numbers of two popular brands are found in Color Keys) or four-ply worsted-weight yarn for stitching on 7-count canvas. There are about 42 yards per ounce of plastic canvas yarn and 50 yards per ounce of worsted-weight yarn.

Worsted-weight yarn is widely available and comes in wool, acrylic, cotton and blends. If you decide to use worsted-weight yarn, choose 100% acrylic for best coverage. Select worsted-weight yarn by color instead of the color names or numbers found in the Color Keys. Projects stitched with worsted-weight yarn often "fuzz" after use. "Fuzz" can be removed by shaving with a fabric shaver to make your project look new again.

Plastic canvas yarn comes in over 60 colors and is a favorite of many plastic canvas designers. These yarns "wear" well both while stitching and in the finished product. When buying plastic canvas yarn, shop using the color names or numbers found in the Color Keys, or select colors of your choice.

Happy Stitching!

Cutting Canvas

Follow all Cutting Instructions, Notes and labels above graphs to cut canvas. Each piece is labeled with a letter of the alphabet. Square-sided pieces are cut according to hole count, and some may not have graphs.

Unlike sewing patterns, graphs are not designed to be used as actual patterns but rather as counting, cutting and stitching guides. Therefore, graphs may not be actual size. Count the holes on the graph (see Marking & Counting Tools on page 6), mark your canvas to match, then cut. Trim off the nubs close to the bar, and trim all corners diagonally.

If you accidentally cut or tear a bar or two on your canvas, don't worry! Boo-boos can usually be repaired in one of several ways: heat the tip of a metal skewer and melt the canvas back together; glue torn bars with a tiny drop of craft glue, Super Glue® or hot glue; or reinforce the torn section with a separate piece of canvas placed at the back of your work. When reinforcing with extra canvas, stitch through both thicknesses.

For More Information

Sometimes even the most experienced needlecrafters can find themselves having trouble following instructions. If you have difficulty completing your project, write to:
Plastic Canvas Editors, *The Needlecraft Shop*, 23 Old Pecan Road, Big Sandy, Texas 75755.

Stitching the Canvas

Stitching Instructions for each section are found after the Cutting Instructions. First, refer to the illustrations of basic stitches to familiarize yourself with the stitches used. Illustrations will be found near the graphs for pieces worked using special stitches. Follow the numbers on the tiny graph beside the illustration to make each stitch — bring your needle up from the back of the work on odd numbers and down through the front of the work on the even numbers.

Before beginning, read the Stitching Instructions to get an overview of what you'll be doing. You'll find that some pieces are stitched using colors and stitches indicated on graphs, and for other pieces, you will be told which color and stitch to use to cover the entire piece.

Cut yarn lengths no longer than 18" to prevent fraying. Thread needle; do not tie a knot in the end. Bring your needle up through the canvas from the back, leaving a short length of yarn on the wrong side of the canvas. As you begin to stitch, work over this short length of yarn. If you are beginning with Continental Stitches, leave a 1" length, but if you are working longer stitches, leave a longer length.

In order for graph colors to contrast well, graph colors may not match yarn colors. For instance, a light yellow may have been selected to represent the metallic cord color gold, or a light blue may represent white yarn.

When following a graph showing several colors, you may want to work all the stitches of one color at the same time. Some stitchers prefer to work with several colors at once by threading each on a separate needle and letting the yarn not being used hang on the wrong side of the work. Either way, remember that strands of yarn run across the wrong side of the work may show through the stitches from the front.

As you stitch, try to maintain an even tension on the yarn. Loose stitches will look uneven, and tight stitches will let the canvas show through. If your yarn twists as you work, you may want to let your needle and yarn hang and untwist occasionally.

When you end a section of stitching or finish a thread, weave the yarn through the back side of your last few stitches, then trim it off.

Construction & Assembly

After all pieces of an item needing assembly are stitched, you will find the order of assembly is listed in the Stitching Instructions and sometimes illustrated in diagrams found with the graphs. For best results, join pieces in the order written. Refer to the Stitch Key and to the directives near the graphs for precise attachments.

Finishing Tips

To combat glue strings when using a hot glue gun, practice a swirling motion as you work. After placing the drop of glue on your work, lift the gun slightly and swirl to break the stream of glue, as if you were making an ice cream cone. Have a cup of water handy when gluing. For those times when you'll need to touch the glue, first dip your finger into the water just enough to dampen it. This will minimize the glue sticking to your finger, and it will cool and set the glue more quickly.

To attach beads, use a bit more glue to form a cup around the bead. If too much shows after drying, use a craft knife to trim off excess glue.

Scotchguard® or other fabric protectors may be used on your finished projects. However, avoid using a permanent marker if you plan to use a fabric protector, and be sure to remove all other markings before stitching. Fabric protectors can cause markings to bleed, staining yarn.

Embroidery Stitch Guide

FRENCH KNOT is usually used as an embroidery stitch to add detail. Can be made in one hole or over a bar. If dot on graph is in hole, come up and go down with needle in same hole. If dot is across a bar, come up in one hole and go down one hole over.

BACKSTITCH is usually used as an embroidery stitch to outline or add detail. Stitches can be any length and can go in any direction.

STRAIGHT STITCH is usually used as an embroidery stitch to add detail. Stitches can be any length and can go in any direction. Looks like Backstitch, except stitches may not touch.

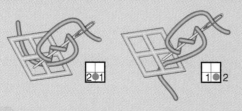

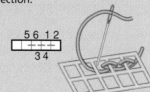

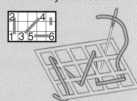

Stitch Guide

CONTINENTAL STITCH

can be used to stitch designs or fill in background areas.

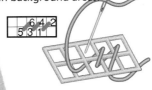

REVERSE CONTINENTAL STITCH

LONG STITCH can be used to stitch designs or fill in background areas. Can be stitched over two or more bars.

ALTERNATING SCOTCH STITCH (OVER 4 BARS)

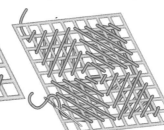

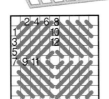

SCOTCH STITCH (OVER 3 BARS)

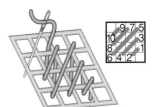

ALTERNATING SLANTED GOBELIN STITCH

SCOTCH STITCH (OVER 4 BARS)

LARK'S HEAD KNOT

Step 1   Step 2

SLANTED GOBELIN STITCH can be used to stitch designs or fill in background areas. Can be stitched over two or more bars in vertical or horizontal rows.

WHIPSTITCH

is used to join two or more pieces together.

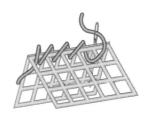

OVERCAST STITCH is used to finish edges. Stitch two or three times in corners for complete coverage.

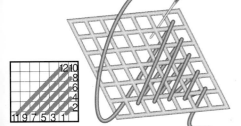

CROSS STITCH can be used as a needlepoint stitch on plastic canvas alone, or as an embroidery stitch, stitched over background stitches with contrasting yarn or floss.

RUNNING STITCH

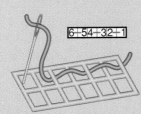

SATIN STITCH

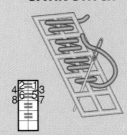

LAZY DAISY STITCH

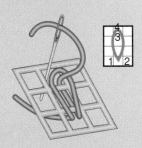

By Renee Stewart

Birthday Party

BIRTHDAY BANNER

SIZE: HAPPY is 5½" x 18⅞"; BIRTHDAY is 5½" x 30¼".

MATERIALS: 2½ sheets of 7-count plastic canvas; Six-strand embroidery floss (for amount see Color Key on page 14); Worsted-weight or plastic canvas yarn (for amounts see Color Key).

CUTTING INSTRUCTIONS: Graphs on pages 14-17.
A: For letter sections, cut thirteen 24 x 36 holes.
B: For hangers, cut four according to graph.

STITCHING INSTRUCTIONS:

NOTE: B pieces are unworked.

1: Using colors indicated and Continental Stitch, work A pieces according to graphs. Fill in uncoded areas using colors shown in photo and Continental Stitch. Using six strands brown floss and Straight Stitch, embroider balloon strings as indicated on graphs. For hangers, with pink, green, dusty blue and yellow, Overcast unfinished edges of one B piece in each color.

2: With matching colors, Overcast unfinished edges of A pieces, connecting hangers and letter sections as you work as shown.

BIRTHDAY CAKE BOX

SIZE: 4¾" tall x 9½" across.

MATERIALS: Two sheets of 12" x 18" or larger stiff 7-count plastic canvas; Three 9½" plastic canvas circles; Craft glue or glue gun; Six-strand embroidery floss (for amount see Color Key on page 17); Worsted-weight or plastic canvas yarn (for amounts see Color Key).

CUTTING INSTRUCTIONS: Graphs, illustration and diagram on pages 16-17.
A: For box sides, cut two 31 x 99 holes (no graph).
B: For box bottom, from one canvas circle, trim off one row of holes (192 holes around–no graph).
C: For box side lining, cut two 30 x 96 holes (no graph).
D: For box bottom lining, from one canvas circle, trim off two rows of holes (188 holes around – no graph).

CELEBRATION GIFTS

E: For lid top, use one canvas circle.

F: For lid lip, cut two according to graph.

G: For letters, cut correct amount for spelling of HAPPY BIRTHDAY, according to graphs.

H: For balloons, cut six according to graph.

STITCHING INSTRUCTIONS:

NOTE: G pieces are unworked.

1: For box, using colors indicated and Continental Stitch, work A pieces according to Box Side Stitch Pattern Guide, overlapping three holes at ends as you work (see Overlap Illustration), forming cylinder (repeat pattern four times). Using white and Slanted Gobelin Stitch over two bars, work B piece, starting at outside edge and working toward center.

2: Holding wrong sides together, with white, Whipstitch A and B pieces together, forming box. Whipstitch unworked C pieces together at short ends,

forming cylinder. Whipstitch C pieces to unworked D piece, forming box lining; place inside box (see Cake Assembly Diagram), and Whipstitch unfinished top edges of box and lining together.

3: For lid, using yellow for outside row and white for remaining rows, work Slanted Gobelin Stitch over two bars on E piece. Using colors and stitches indicated, work F pieces according to graph, overlapping three holes at ends as you work, forming cylinder. Fill in uncoded area using white and Continental Stitch. With yellow, Whipstitch E and F together (see diagram); Overcast unfinished edges.

4: With colors of choice, Overcast unfinished edges on G pieces. Using colors of choice and Continental Stitch, work H pieces; with matching colors, Overcast unfinished edges.

5: Glue letters and balloons to lid as shown in photo. Using brown floss and Straight Stitch, embroider balloon strings as shown in photo. ▭

Celebrate with merry balloons and bright colors! The festive banner sets a happy scene, while the birthday cake box holds a gift or birthday mementos.

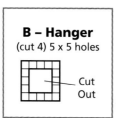

B – Hanger
(cut 4) 5 x 5 holes

— Cut Out

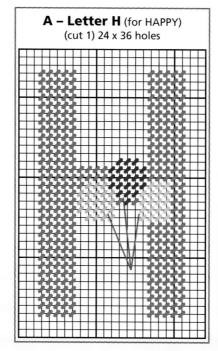

A – Letter H (for HAPPY)
(cut 1) 24 x 36 holes

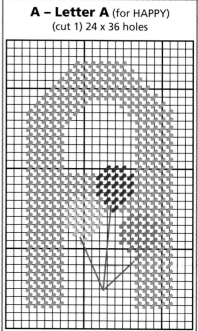

A – Letter A (for HAPPY)
(cut 1) 24 x 36 holes

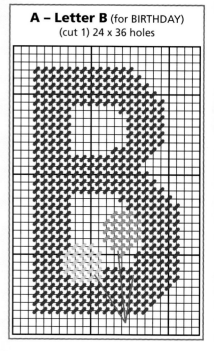

A – Letter B (for BIRTHDAY)
(cut 1) 24 x 36 holes

COLOR KEY: Birthday Banner

Embroidery floss			AMOUNT
Brown			14 yds.

Worsted-weight	Nylon Plus™	Need-loft™	YARN AMOUNT
Green	#58	#28	42 yds.
Royal	#09	#32	35 yds.
Yellow	#26	#57	35 yds.
Dusty Blue	#38	#34	30 yds.
Lt. Green	#28	#26	30 yds.
Pink	#11	#07	30 yds.
Red	#19	#02	30 yds.
Lavender	#22	#45	25 yds.

STITCH KEY:

— Backstitch/Straight Stitch

A – Letter P (for HAPPY)
(cut 1) 24 x 36 holes

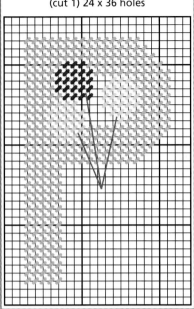

A – Letter P (for HAPPY)
(cut 1) 24 x 36 holes

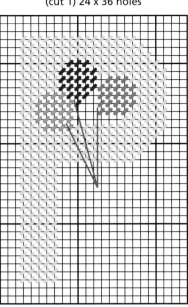

A – Letter Y (for HAPPY)
(cut 1) 24 x 36 holes

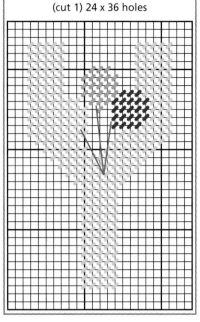

A – Letter I (for BIRTHDAY)
(cut 1) 24 x 36 holes

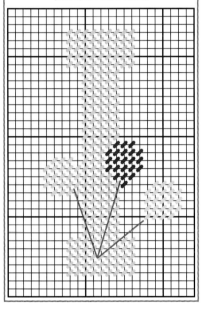

A – Letter R (for BIRTHDAY)
(cut 1) 24 x 36 holes

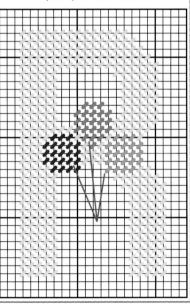

A – Letter T (for BIRTHDAY)
(cut 1) 24 x 36 holes

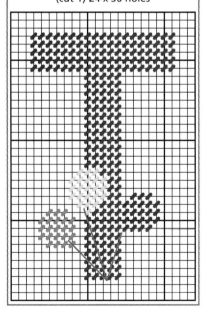

A – Letter H (for BIRTHDAY)
(cut 1) 24 x 36 holes

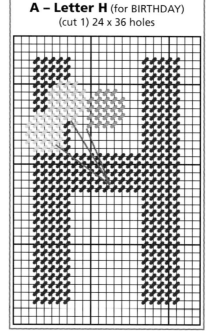

A – Letter D (for BIRTHDAY)
(cut 1) 24 x 36 holes

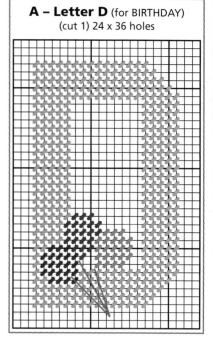

G – Letters
Cut out gray areas.

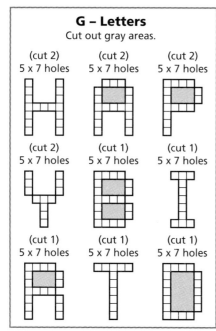

(cut 2) 5 x 7 holes — H
(cut 2) 5 x 7 holes — A
(cut 2) 5 x 7 holes — P
(cut 2) 5 x 7 holes — Y
(cut 1) 5 x 7 holes — B
(cut 1) 5 x 7 holes — I
(cut 1) 5 x 7 holes — R
(cut 1) 5 x 7 holes — T
(cut 1) 5 x 7 holes — D

COLOR KEY: Birthday Banner

Embroidery floss			AMOUNT
Brown			14 yds.

Worsted-weight	Nylon Plus™	Need-loft™	YARN AMOUNT
Green	#58	#28	42 yds.
Royal	#09	#32	35 yds.
Yellow	#26	#57	35 yds.
Dusty Blue	#38	#34	30 yds.
Lt. Green	#28	#26	30 yds.
Pink	#11	#07	30 yds.
Red	#19	#02	30 yds.
Lavender	#22	#45	25 yds.

STITCH KEY:
— Backstitch/Straight Stitch

H – Balloon
(cut 6) 6 x 6 holes

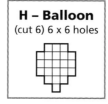

A – Letter A (for BIRTHDAY)
(cut 1) 24 x 36 holes

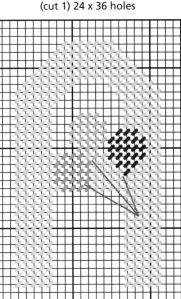

A – Letter Y (for BIRTHDAY)
(cut 1) 24 x 36 holes

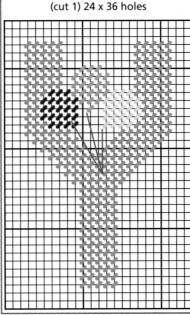

F – Lid Lip #1
(cut 1) 10 x 120 holes

F – Lid Lip #2
(cut 1) 10 x 84 holes

Overlap Illustration

Box Side Stitch Pattern Guide
(repeat pattern 4 times around)

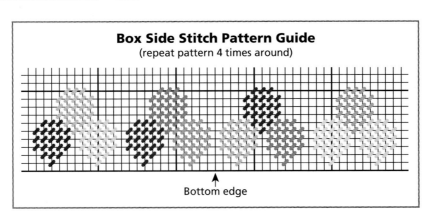

↑
Bottom edge

COLOR KEY: Birthday Cake Box

Embroidery floss			AMOUNT
Brown			14 yds.

Worsted-weight	Nylon Plus™	Need-loft™	YARN AMOUNT
Yellow	#26	#57	35 yds.
Dusty Blue	#38	#34	8 yds.
Green	#58	#28	8 yds.
Lt. Green	#28	#26	8 yds.
Pink	#11	#07	8 yds.
Red	#19	#02	8 yds.
Royal	#09	#32	8 yds.
Lavender	#22	#45	6 yds.
White	#01	#41	6 yds.

Cake Assembly Diagram

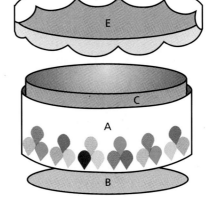

CELEBRATION GIFTS

Whip up a batch of these whimsical little baskets to hold candy, balloons and other tiny party goodies.

By Vicki Watkins

Basket Buddies

CELEBRATION GIFTS

SIZE: Baskets are 1⅜" x 1⅝", not including handles and motifs.

MATERIALS FOR SET OF 6: ½ sheet of white 7-count plastic canvas; Scraps of green, tan and brown 7-count plastic canvas; Six-strand embroidery floss (for amounts see Color Key); Worsted-weight or plastic canvas yarn (for amounts see Color Key).

CUTTING INSTRUCTIONS:
A: For basket sides, cut twelve from white and four from each remaining color 8 x 10 holes (no graph).
B: For basket bottoms, cut three from white and one from each remaining color 10 x 10 holes (no graph).
C: For handles, cut three from white and one from each remaining color 2 x 26 holes (no graph).
D: For motifs, cut one each (Bunny, Snowman and Kitty from white; Strawberry from green; Puppy from tan; Bear from brown) according to graphs.

STITCHING INSTRUCTIONS:

1: Using colors and stitches indicated, work D pieces according to graphs. Fill in uncoded areas of Bunny, Snowman and Kitty using white, Strawberry using red and Bear using cinnamon and Continental Stitch. Using maple and Continental Stitch, work Puppy. With white for Kitty and Bunny ears, cinnamon for Bear ears and with matching colors, Overcast unfinished edges of D pieces.

2: Using six strands floss in colors indicated, Backstitch, Straight Stitch and French Knot, embroider detail as indicated on graphs.

3: Using two strands yellow floss and French Knot, embroider one seed in each hole on red section of Strawberry as shown in photo.

4: Matching yarn and canvas colors, Whipstitch bas-

ket pieces together, forming three white, one green, one tan and one brown basket as shown in photo. Overcast unfinished top edges of baskets, Whipstitching short ends of matching color handles to basket sides. Tack motifs to basket sides as shown.

COLOR KEY: Basket Buddies

Embroidery floss	AMOUNT
■ Black	1 yd.
□ Yellow	1 yd.
▨ Pink	½ yd.
▨ Gray	½ yd.
■ Red	⅓ yd.

Worsted-weight	Nylon Plus™	Need-loft™	YARN AMOUNT
□ White	#01	#41	12 yds.
□ Maple	#35	#13	5 yds.
□ Cinnamon	#44	#14	4 yds.
▨ Fern	#57	#23	2½ yds.
■ Black	#02	#00	2 yds.
□ Red	#19	#02	2 yds.
▨ Pink	#11	#07	1 yd.
▨ Forest	#32	#29	½ yd.
▨ Sail Blue	#04	#35	½ yd.
▨ Sand	#47	#16	½ yd.
▨ Orange	#17	#58	¼ yd.

STITCH KEY:
— Backstitch/Straight Stitch
● French Knot

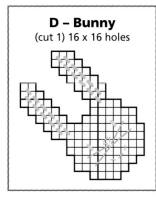

D – Bunny
(cut 1) 16 x 16 holes

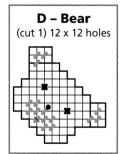

D – Bear
(cut 1) 12 x 12 holes

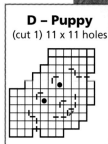

D – Puppy
(cut 1) 11 x 11 holes

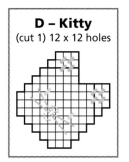

D – Kitty
(cut 1) 12 x 12 holes

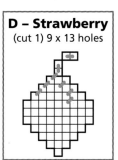

D – Strawberry
(cut 1) 9 x 13 holes

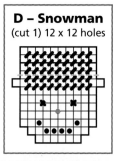

D – Snowman
(cut 1) 12 x 12 holes

CELEBRATION GIFTS

SIZE: Board is 11¼" x 11¾"; each Playing Piece is 1" square.

MATERIALS: Two sheets of 12" x 18" or larger 7-count plastic canvas; ¾ yd. off-white ¼" satin ribbon; 2" sawtooth hanger (optional); Craft glue or glue gun; Worsted-weight or plastic canvas yarn (for amounts see Color Key).

CUTTING INSTRUCTIONS:
A: For Board, cut two according to graph.
B: For Playing Pieces, cut twenty-four according to graph.

STITCHING INSTRUCTIONS:

NOTE: One A piece is unworked for backing.

1: Using colors and stitches indicated, work one A according to graph. Fill in uncoded areas using dk. red and Continental Stitch. Holding backing A to wrong side of worked piece, with matching colors, Whipstitch together. If desired, glue sawtooth hanger to back.

2: Using dk. red, green and Continental Stitch, work twelve B pieces in each color. With matching colors, Overcast unfinished edges of Playing Pieces. To store, thread Playing Pieces on ribbon; tie ends in a bow.

Add a dash of country charm to your home with this delectable apple game board set. String checkers on jute or string and hang on stem.

By Michele Wilcox

Apple Checkers

COLOR KEY: Apple Checkers

Worsted-weight	Nylon Plus™	Need-loft™	YARN AMOUNT
☐ Dk. Red	#20	#01	40 yds.
■ Dusty Blue	#38	#34	18 yds.
■ Eggshell	#24	#39	18 yds.
■ Green	#58	#28	14 yds.
■ Cinnamon	#44	#14	2½ yds.

B – Playing Piece
(cut 24) 6 x 6 holes
Cut out gray area.

A – Board
(cut 2) 74 x 77 holes

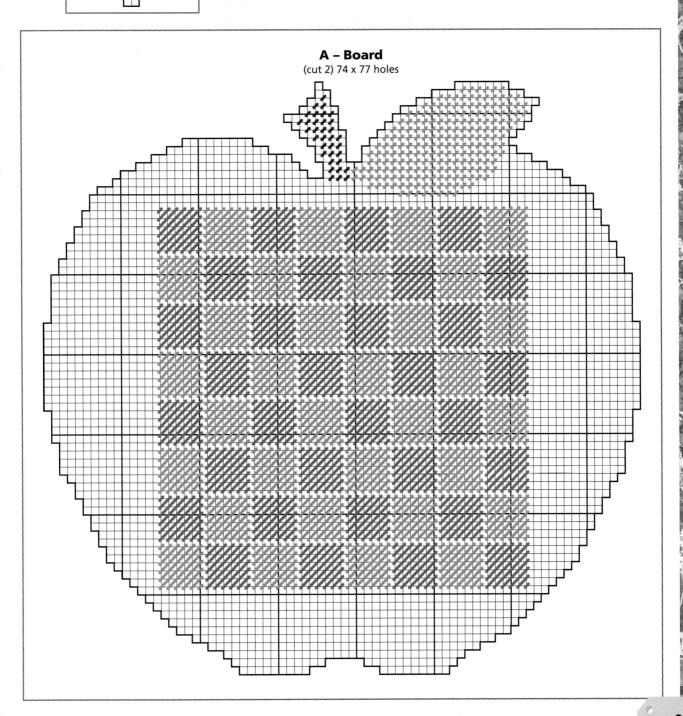

By Trudy Bath Smith

Dress Up

SIZE: 10⅝" tall; holds a boutique-style tissue box.

MATERIALS: 1¾ sheets of 7-count plastic canvas; 3" x 4" oval mirror or craft foil; 12" pink rattail cord; Six gold 8-mm. filigree beads; Velcro® closure (optional); Craft glue or glue gun; Worsted-weight or plastic canvas yarn (for amounts see Color Key on page 24).

CUTTING INSTRUCTIONS: Graphs on page 24.
A: For front, cut one according to graph.
B: For back and back lining, cut one each according to graph.
C: For ends, cut two according to graph.
D: For top, cut one 30 x 37 holes (no graph).
E: For bottom and flap, cut one 29 x 37 holes (no graph) and one according to graph.

STITCHING INSTRUCTIONS:

NOTE: E pieces are unworked.

1: Using colors and stitches indicated, work A, one B and C pieces according to graphs, continuing established pattern across solid end. Fill in uncoded areas of A and mirror area of worked B using white and Continental Stitch, leaving indicated area of back unworked. With white, Overcast unfinished cutout edges of end. Using white and Slanted Gobelin Stitch over three bars, work D in horizontal rows across length of piece.

2: Holding unworked B to wrong side of worked piece, with matching colors, Whipstitch mirror and post areas together as indicated on graph. With white, Whipstitch unworked E pieces together at one matching long edge. Working through all thicknesses,

Whipstitch opposite edge of bottom to back as indicated and according to Dress Up Assembly Diagram. Whipstitch A, back, C and D pieces together; Overcast unfinished edges of dresser.

3: Glue beads to front as indicated. Glue mirror to back and cord around mirror as shown in photo. If desired, glue closure to flap and inside of front. ▱

Dress Up Assembly Diagram

CELEBRATION GIFTS

Surprise the birthday girl with a feminine, miniature dresser that's really a tissue cover! It's complete with mirror and "gilded" drawer pulls.

B – Back & Lining (cut 1 each) 37 x 70 holes

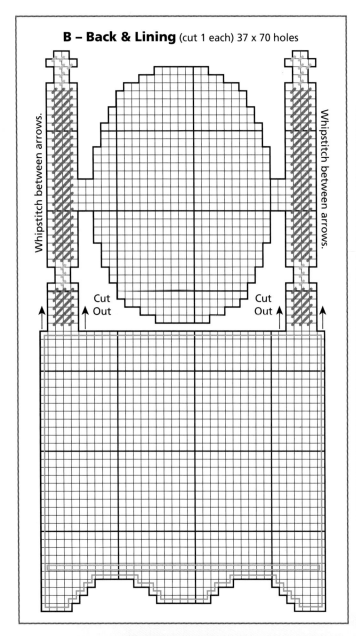

Whipstitch between arrows.

Whipstitch between arrows.

Cut Out

Cut Out

E – Flap (cut 1) 5 x 37 holes

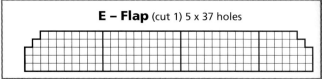

A – Front (cut 1) 35 x 37 holes

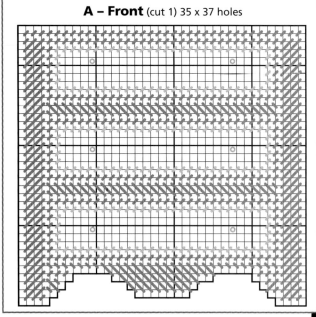

C – End (cut 2) 30 x 35 holes

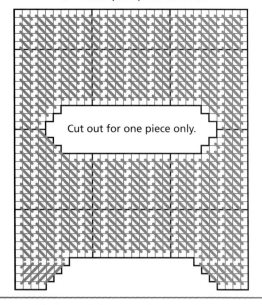

Cut out for one piece only.

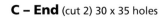

COLOR KEY: Dress Up

Worsted-weight	Nylon Plus™	Need-loft™	YARN AMOUNT
White	#01	#41	60 yds.
Pink	#11	#07	6 yds.

STITCH KEY:
- Unworked Area
- Bottom Attachment
- Bead Placement

SWEETHEART GIFTS

CELEBRATION GIFTS

Little Sweethearts

Your favorite little Miss will adore her very own dainty bow-trimmed hairbrush.

HEART BRUSH
By Pamela Noel

SIZE: 4¼" x 7⅞".

MATERIALS: One sheet of stiff 7-count plastic canvas; ¼ yd. white ⅜" satin ribbon; 21 craft or ice cream sticks; Clear silicon gel; Craft glue or glue gun; Worsted-weight or plastic canvas yarn (for amounts see Color Key).

CUTTING INSTRUCTIONS: Graphs continued on page 28.
Graphs continued on page 28.
  A: For front and back, cut one each according to graphs.
  B: For bristle pad, cut one according to graph.
  C: For bristles, cut number indicated according to graphs.

STITCHING INSTRUCTIONS:

NOTE: B and C pieces are unworked.

1: Using colors and stitches indicated, work A pieces according to graphs, leaving uncoded area of front unworked.

NOTE: Steps 2-5 must be done in one sitting.

2: With wrong side of front A facing up, insert C pieces down through unworked rows of holes according to Bristle Assembly Diagram.

3: To set bristles in place, squeeze a generous amount of silicone gel over wrong side of front across bristle bars. Use enough gel to fill in spaces between bars and to secure bristles to front without forcing gel through to right side. Cover immediately with unworked B, and generously squeeze gel over bristle pad. Use craft stick to force gel through holes to fill in spaces between bristle bars and pad.

4: To give added strength to handle, place one craft stick lengthwise over handle area on wrong side. Holding A pieces wrong sides together with pad and craft stick between, with red, Whipstitch together.

5: Place one craft stick between each row of bristles. Wrap yarn around brush and craft sticks to hold in place. Let dry about 12 hours before removing sticks.

6: Tie ribbon into a bow; trim ends. Glue to back as shown in photo. 🗨

Bristle Assembly Diagram

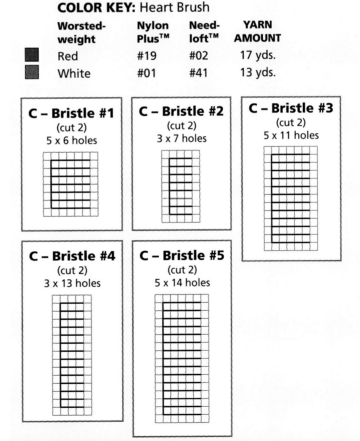

Unworked Area on Front A

COLOR KEY: Heart Brush

	Worsted-weight	Nylon Plus™	Need-loft™	YARN AMOUNT
■	Red	#19	#02	17 yds.
■	White	#01	#41	13 yds.

C – Bristle #1
(cut 2)
5 x 6 holes

C – Bristle #2
(cut 2)
3 x 7 holes

C – Bristle #3
(cut 2)
5 x 11 holes

C – Bristle #4
(cut 2)
3 x 13 holes

C – Bristle #5
(cut 2)
5 x 14 holes

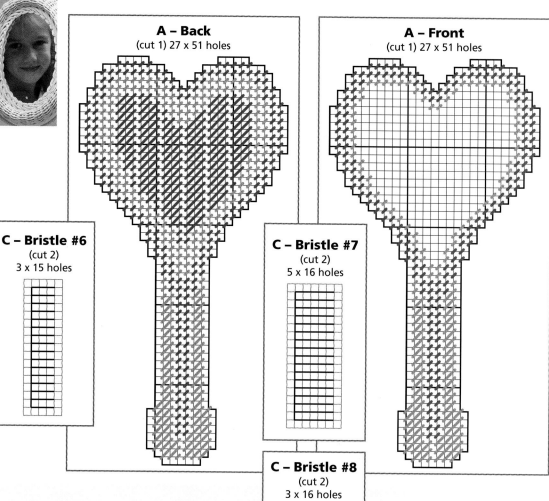

A – Back
(cut 1) 27 x 51 holes

A – Front
(cut 1) 27 x 51 holes

C – Bristle #6
(cut 2)
3 x 15 holes

C – Bristle #7
(cut 2)
5 x 16 holes

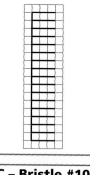

C – Bristle #8
(cut 2)
3 x 16 holes

COLOR KEY: Heart Brush

Worsted-weight	Nylon Plus™	Need-loft™	YARN AMOUNT
Red	#19	#02	17 yds.
White	#01	#41	13 yds.

C – Bristle #9
(cut 2)
5 x 17 holes

C – Bristle #11
(cut 1)
5 x 19 holes

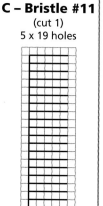

B – Bristle Pad
(cut 1)
21 x 25 holes

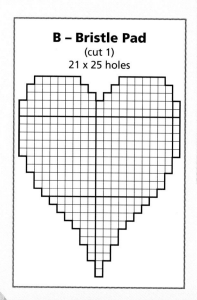

C – Bristle #10
(cut 2)
3 x 18 holes

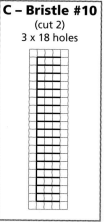

CELEBRATION GIFTS

PARTY FAVORS
By Kathryn Bath Schaller

SIZE: About 3½" x 4½".

MATERIALS: Scraps of 7-count plastic canvas; 9" black ⅛" satin ribbon; One red 6-mm. chenille stem; Craft glue or glue gun; Worsted-weight or plastic canvas yarn (for amounts see Color Key).

CUTTING INSTRUCTIONS:
A: For heart, cut two according to graph.
B: For hands, cut four according to graph.
C: For feet, cut four according to graph.

STITCHING INSTRUCTIONS:

1: Using red and Continental Stitch, work one A for back, and work remaining A piece according to graph. Fill in uncoded areas of front A and work B and C pieces using white and Continental Stitch.

NOTE: Cut chenille stem into two 2" and two 2½" lengths.

2: For each arm, holding two matching B pieces wrong sides together with 2" chenille stem between as indicated, with white, Whipstitch together. For each leg, repeat as for arms using C pieces. Holding A pieces wrong sides together with arms and legs between as shown in photo, Whipstitch together.

3: Tie ribbon into a bow; trim ends. Glue to heart as shown. ▱

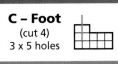

A – Heart
(cut 2) 12 x 12 holes

C – Foot
(cut 4)
3 x 5 holes

B – Hand
(cut 4)
4 x 4 holes

COLOR KEY: Party Favors			
Worsted-weight	**Nylon Plus™**	**Need-loft™**	**YARN AMOUNT**
■ Red	#19	#02	4 yds.
□ White	#01	#41	4 yds.

STITCH KEY:
— Chenille Stem Attachment

Clever heart party favors sport boy and girl bows, and they bend to sit or stand.

CELEBRATION GIFTS

SIZE: 3¼" x 3½" x 6⅛" long, not including handle.

MATERIALS: One sheet of 7-count plastic canvas; Craft glue or glue gun; Worsted-weight or plastic canvas yarn (for amounts see Color Key).

CUTTING INSTRUCTIONS:

A: For sides, cut two 15 x 35 holes.
B: For ends, cut two 15 x 19 holes.
C: For bottom, cut one 19 x 35 holes (no graph).
D: For wheels, cut four according to graph.
E: For handle extension, cut one according to graph.
F: For handle, cut one according to graph.

STITCHING INSTRUCTIONS:

1: Using colors and stitches indicated, work A, B, D, E and F pieces according to graphs. Using beige and Slanted Gobelin Stitch over two bars, work C in vertical rows across width of piece.

2: Holding right side of bottom facing in, with camel, Whipstitch A, B and C pieces together, forming wagon. With camel, Overcast unfinished edges of D-F pieces. Whipstitch handle and handle extension together as indicated on graphs.

3: Glue wheels to wagon as indicated, and holding right side of extension facing up, glue to underside of one end as shown in photo.

COLOR KEY: My Little Wagon

Worsted-weight	Nylon Plus™	Need-loft™	YARN AMOUNT
Beige	#43	#40	40 yds.
Camel	#34	#43	18 yds.
Red	#20	#01	15 yds.

STITCH KEY:

☐ Wheel Placement

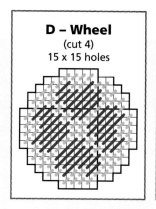

D – Wheel
(cut 4)
15 x 15 holes

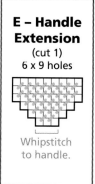

E – Handle Extension
(cut 1)
6 x 9 holes

Whipstitch to handle.

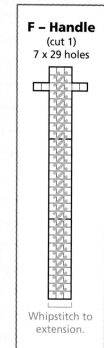

F – Handle
(cut 1)
7 x 29 holes

Whipstitch to extension.

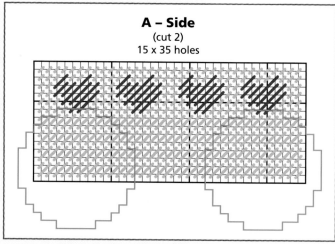

A – Side
(cut 2)
15 x 35 holes

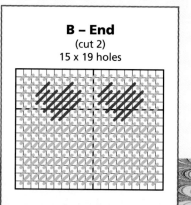

B – End
(cut 2)
15 x 19 holes

CELEBRATION GIFTS

By Lilo Fruehwirth

My Little Wagon

Trimmed with pretty red hearts, this adorable wagon makes a captivating tabletop accent when filled with Spanish moss and artificial greenery.

CELEBRATION GIFTS

SIZE: Tissue Cover snugly covers a long family-size Kleenex® tissue box; Bathroom Tissue Holder is 4½" x 5⅛" x 13⅝" and holds three rolls of tissue; Organizer is 8¼" x 8¼" x 5¾" tall.

MATERIALS: Seven sheets of 7–count plastic canvas; 1 yd. white 1" pregathered lace; 1 yd. white ¼" satin ribbon; ⅓ yd. white elastic cord; ¾" yd. white ¾" eyelet edging; Three white ¾" satin ribbon roses; One 20-mm. wooden bead; 2" sawtooth hanger; Craft glue or glue gun; Worsted-weight or plastic canvas yarn (for amount see Color Key on page 35).

CUTTING INSTRUCTIONS: Graphs and diagrams on pages 34-37.

A: For Holder front and back, cut one according to graph and one 33 x 89 holes (no back graph).
B: For Holder door, cut one according to graph.
C: For Holder sides, cut two 29 x 89 holes (no graph).
D: For Holder top and bottom, cut one each 29 x 33 holes (no graphs).

E: For Tissue Cover sides and ends, cut two each according to graphs.
F: For Tissue Cover top, cut one according to graph.
G: For Organizer lid top, cut one according to graph.
H: For Organizer lid sides, cut one 6 x 62 holes, two 6 x 53 holes and two 6 x 9 holes (no graphs).
I: For Organizer box front, cut two according to graph.
J: For Organizer box long and short sides, cut four 35 x 51 holes and four 8 x 35 holes (no graphs).
K: For Organizer box bottom, cut

By Machelle Sustaita

Vanity Cover-Ups

CELEBRATION GIFTS

Lacy tissue cover,
bathroom tissue holder
and handy corner
toiletry organizer all
feature heart cutouts and
are trimmed with lace,
ribbon and satin roses.

two according to graph.

L: For Organizer box dividers, cut one 24 x 34 holes and two 29 x 34 holes (no graphs).

NOTES: Cut three 12" lengths of ribbon and three 12" lengths of pregathered lace. For each bow, tie one 12" length of ribbon into a bow. Gather one 12" length of lace and glue around stem of one satin ribbon rose. Glue bow to center of lace.

BATHROOM TISSUE HOLDER STITCHING INSTRUCTIONS:

1: Using white and stitches indicated, work front A and B pieces according to graphs, and work back A, C and D pieces according to Holder Stitch Pattern Guide. Overcast unfinished cutout edges of front A and B pieces.

NOTE: Cut one 24" length of white.

2: With 24" strand of white, bring needle up through wrong side of front A at ▲ holes, through bead, then back down through neighboring ▲ hole. Repeat as above; knot and trim ends on wrong side to secure. With 12" strand of elastic cord, bring needle up through wrong side of B at ◆ hole, then back down through neighboring ◆ hole. Repeat as above, leaving a 2" loop for closure; knot and trim ends on wrong side to secure.

3: With white, Whipstitch A-D pieces together according to Holder Assembly Diagram; Overcast unfinished edges. Glue sawtooth hanger to back and glue one bow (see **NOTE** below Cutting Instructions) to

front as shown in photo.

TISSUE COVER STITCHING INSTRUCTIONS:

1: Using white and stitches indicated, work E and F pieces according to graphs; Overcast unfinished cutout edges.

2: With white, Whipstitch E and F pieces together, forming cover; Overcast unfinished edges. Glue one bow (see **NOTE** below Cutting Instructions) to front as shown.

ORGANIZER STITCHING INSTRUCTIONS:

NOTE: K and L pieces are unworked.

1: Using white and stitches indicated, work G and one I according to graphs; work H pieces according to Organizer Lid Side Stitch Pattern Guide. Work two long J pieces according to Organizer Box Long Side Stitch Pattern Guide, and work two short J pieces according to Organizer Box Short Side Stitch Pattern Guide. (**NOTE:** For lid sides and box short sides, pattern will not end evenly.)

2: With white, Whipstitch G and H pieces together according to Organizer Lid Assembly Diagram; Overcast unfinished edges. Whipstitch unworked L pieces together according to Organizer Box Assembly diagram; Whipstitch dividers to unworked I and one unworked K as indicated on graphs.

3: Holding matching I, J and K pieces together and working through all thicknesses, Whipstitch together according to Organizer Box Assembly Diagram; Whipstitch unfinished top edges together, and Overcast unfinished top edges of dividers. Tack corners of dividers to box long sides to secure. Glue eyelet lacing around lid sides as shown. Glue one bow (see **NOTE** below Cutting Instructions) to front as shown.

Holder Assembly Diagram

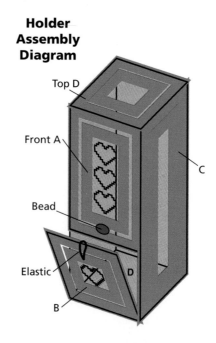

Top D

Front A

Bead

Elastic

B

D

C

34

COLOR KEY: Vanity Cover-Ups

	Worsted-weight	Nylon Plus™	Need-loft™	YARN AMOUNT
■	White	#01	#41	6 oz.

STITCH KEY:
▲ Bead Attachment
♦ Elastic Attachment
☐ Divider Attachment

Organizer Lid Side Stitch Pattern Guide

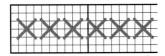

Continue established pattern across each entire piece.

Organizer Box Short Side Stitch Pattern Guide

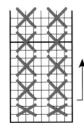

Continue established pattern across each entire piece.

Organizer Box Long Side Stitch Pattern Guide

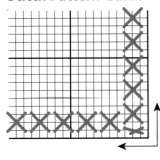

Continue established pattern up and across each entire piece.

Holder Stitch Pattern Guide

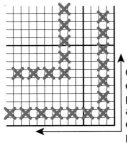

Continue established pattern up and across each entire piece.

B – Holder Door (cut 1) 30 x 33 holes

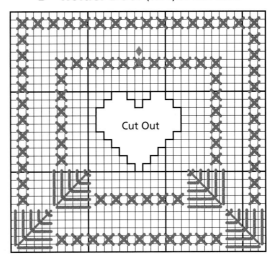

A – Holder Front (cut 1) 33 x 58 holes

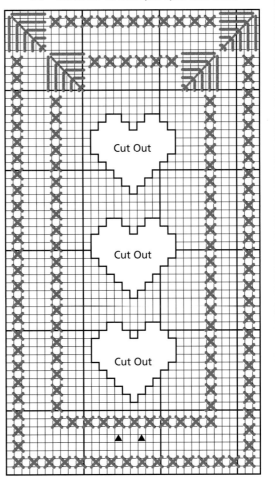

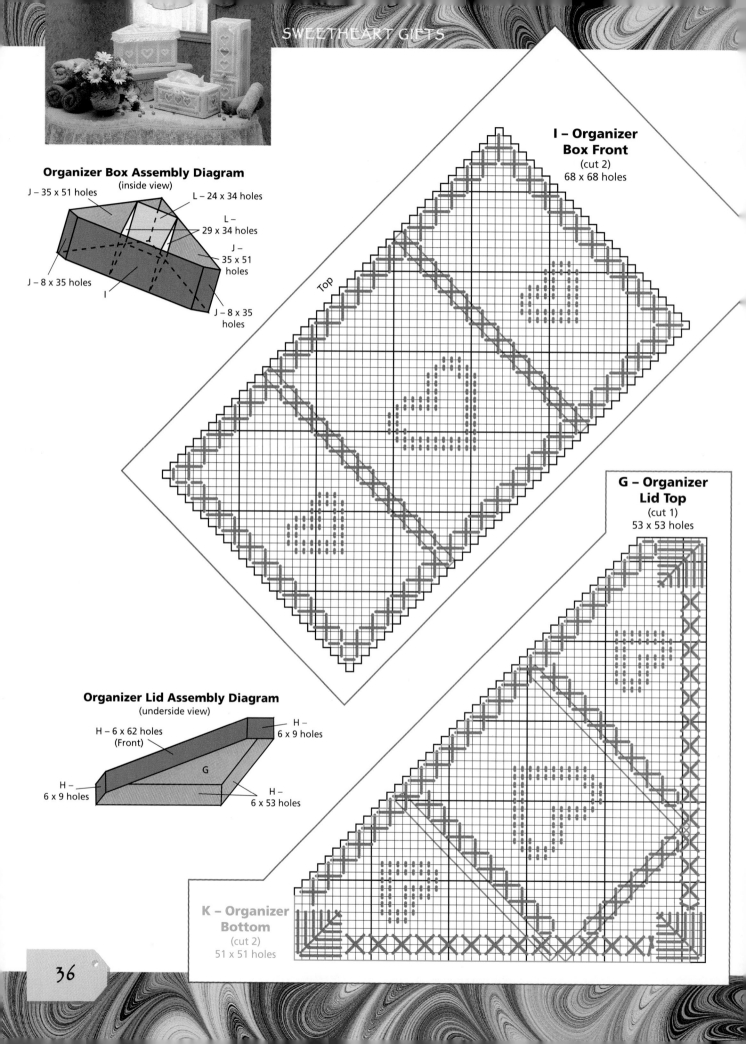

Organizer Box Assembly Diagram
(inside view)

J – 35 x 51 holes

L – 24 x 34 holes

L – 29 x 34 holes

J – 35 x 51 holes

J – 8 x 35 holes

I

J – 8 x 35 holes

I – Organizer Box Front
(cut 2)
68 x 68 holes

Top

G – Organizer Lid Top
(cut 1)
53 x 53 holes

Organizer Lid Assembly Diagram
(underside view)

H – 6 x 62 holes (Front)

H – 6 x 9 holes

H – 6 x 9 holes

G

H – 6 x 53 holes

K – Organizer Bottom
(cut 2)
51 x 51 holes

E – Tissue Cover Side (cut 2) 27 x 63 holes

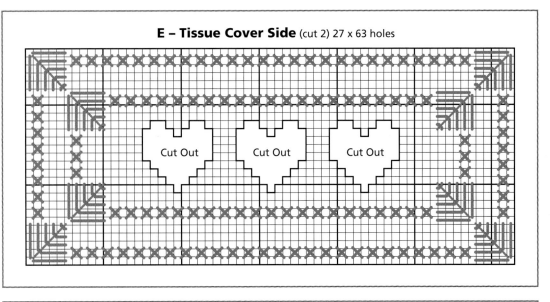

Cut Out   Cut Out   Cut Out

F – Tissue Cover Top (cut 1) 31 x 63 holes

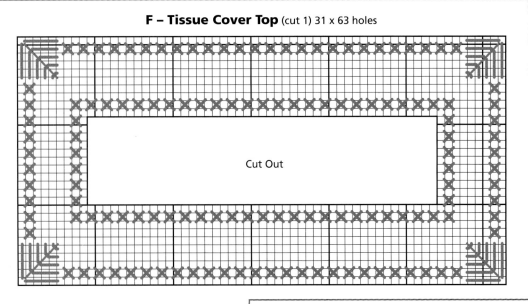

Cut Out

COLOR KEY: Vanity Cover-Ups

Worsted-weight	Nylon Plus™	Need-loft™	YARN AMOUNT
White	#01	#41	6 oz.

STITCH KEY:
▲ Bead Attachment
♦ Elastic Attachment
☐ Divider Attachment

E – Tissue Cover End (cut 2) 27 x 31 holes

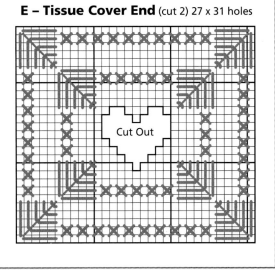

Cut Out

SIZE: Arrangement is about 8" across x 7½" tall.

MATERIALS: Three sheets of 10-count plastic canvas; 3" plastic canvas radial circle; 13 yellow 5-mm. pom-poms; Four 18" lengths of 20-gauge green cloth-covered floral wire; Seven 18" lengths of 18-gauge floral wire; Floral tape; One 2" x 3" floral foam block; 3-ply or sport weight yarn (for amounts see Color Key).

CUTTING INSTRUCTIONS:

A: For vase sides, cut eight according to graph.

B: For vase bottom, use 3" canvas circle (no graph).

C: For center petals, cut thirteen according to graph.

D: For top petals, cut thirteen according to graph.

E: For bottom petals, cut twenty-six according to graph.

F: For calyxes, cut thirteen according to graph.

G: For leaves, cut thirty-nine according to graph.

STITCHING INSTRUCTIONS:

NOTE: B piece is unworked.

1: For vase, using variegated gray and Continental Stitch, work A pieces; easing to fit, Whipstitch side edges together as indicated on graph. Easing to fit, Whipstitch bottom edges and B together; Overcast unfinished edges of vase.

2: Using forest and stitches indicated, work G pieces according to graph. Using forest and Continental Stitch,

By Maria Berenger

Pretty Pansies

Here's a Mother's Day bouquet that will last and last. Capture the classic appeal of fragile pansies in this versatile arrangement.

work F pieces; Overcast unfinished edges of leaves and calyxes.

3: For flowers, using black and Continental Stitch, work C and D pieces according to graphs. Fill in uncoded areas on two of each C and D and work four E pieces using one of the following colors and Continental Stitch; bright pink, gold, lavender, red violet and rose. Fill in uncoded areas of remaining C-E pieces using dk. violet and Continental Stitch. With lt. yellow for points on D pieces as indicated and with matching flower colors, Overcast unfinished edges of C-E pieces.

NOTE: Cut cloth-covered wire into thirty-nine 2" lengths and 18-gauge wire into thirteen 7" lengths.

4: For each stem, wrap top 2" of one 7" wire with tape. Continue wrapping wire, attaching three 2" wires for leaf stems according to Stem Diagram. Thread top of stem through calyx and matching color petals according to Pansy Assembly Diagram, ending evenly with top petal; glue pieces together to secure. Covering stem top, glue one pom-pom to center of each flower. Glue one leaf to each 2" stem.

C – Center Petal
(cut 13)
18 x 18 holes

F – Calyx
(cut 13)
12 x 12 holes
Cut out gray area.

D – Top Petal
(cut 13) 13 x 13 holes

Overcast with lt. yellow.

E – Bottom Petal
(cut 26) 12 x 12 holes

A – Vase Side (cut 8) 21 x 38 holes

Top

Whipstitch between arrows.

G – Leaf
(cut 39)
13 x 13 holes

Stem Diagram

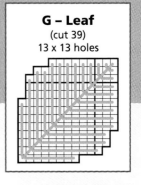

2" Stems

7" Stem

COLOR KEY: Pretty Pansies

3-ply yarn	AMOUNT
▨ Forest	80 yds.
☐ Variegated Gray	70 yds.
■ Black	26 yds.
☐ Bright Pink	20 yds.
☐ Gold	20 yds.
☐ Lavender	20 yds.
☐ Red Violet	20 yds.
☐ Rose	20 yds.
☐ Lt. Yellow	15 yds.
☐ Dk. Violet	10 yds.

STITCH KEY:
o   Petal Attachment

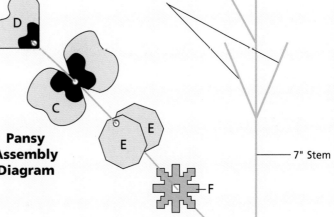

Pansy Assembly Diagram

D

C

E

E

F

SPRINGTIME
CELEBRATIONS

By Trudy Bath Smith

Cottontail Parade

These whimsical bunnies enjoy the blessings of warmer weather! Dressed in overalls and aprons, Mama, Papa and the kids set the mood for a joyful spring.

CELEBRATION GIFTS

SIZE: Bases are 3¼" x 6⅛"; Bunnies are 5½"-7¼" tall.

MATERIALS FOR ONE OF EACH: Five sheets of 7-count plastic canvas; Scrap of 10-count plastic canvas (for Baby); At least 24 silk or paper forget-me-nots; Monofilament fishing line; 12" purple chenille stem; ½ yd. kite string (optional); Two black 2" double-headed flower stamens; Craft glue or glue gun; Worsted-weight or plastic canvas yarn (for amounts see Color Key on page 45). Graphs and illustrations on pages 45-47.

PAPA
CUTTING INSTRUCTIONS:
    A: For base, cut two according to graph.
    B: For body, cut two according to graph.
    C: For foot supports, cut two 3 x 5 holes (no graph).
    D: For butterfly sides, cut two according to graph.

STITCHING INSTRUCTIONS:

1: Using fern and Slanted Gobelin Stitch, work one A according to graph. For grass, using green and Modified Turkey Work (see Stitch Illustration), embroider several loops on right side center of base as shown in photo. Holding unworked A to wrong side of worked piece, with fern, Whipstitch together.

2: Using colors and stitches indicated, work one B and D (one on opposite side of canvas) pieces according to graphs. Using colors indicated, Backstitch and French Knot, embroider facial features and butterfly detail as indicated on graphs.

3: Holding unworked B to wrong side of worked piece, with matching colors, Whipstitch together as indicated. With white, Whipstitch one C to open edges of each foot as indicated; Overcast unfinished edges of feet. Holding D pieces wrong sides together, with black, Whipstitch together as indicated, forming butterfly; with straw, Overcast unfinished edges.

4: Fold one double-headed stamen in half; glue to back of butterfly as shown. Glue butterfly to Papa and Papa to center of base as shown. Glue forget-me-knots to Papa and base as shown.

MAMA
CUTTING INSTRUCTIONS:
    A: For base, cut two according to Papa A graph.
    B: For body, cut two according to graph.
    C: For arms, cut two according to graph.
    D: For body support, cut one 3 x 10 holes (no graph).
    E: For flower pot, cut one according to graph.

STITCHING INSTRUCTIONS:

1: Follow Step 1 of Papa on page 43.

2: Using colors and stitches indicated, work one B, C (one on opposite side of canvas) and E pieces according to graphs. Using colors indicated, Backstitch and French Knot, embroider facial features as indicated on graph. With matching colors, Overcast unfinished edges of C and E pieces.

3: Holding unworked B to wrong side of worked piece, with matching colors, Whipstitch together as indicated. Whipstitch D to open edges of body as indicated; Overcast unfinished edges of dress.

NOTE: Cut one 9" length of lavender.

4: Tie 9" strand of lavender into a bow; trim ends. Glue bow, flower pot and arms to Mama and Mama to center of base as shown.

BOY
CUTTING INSTRUCTIONS:
A: For base, cut two according to Papa A graph.
B: For body, cut two according to graph.
C: For foot supports, cut two 2 x 2 holes (no graph).
D: For balloons, cut two according to graph.

STITCHING INSTRUCTIONS:

1: Follow Step 1 of Papa.

2: Using colors and stitches indicated, work one B and one D according to graphs. Substituting green for watermelon, work remaining D according to graph. Using colors indicated, Backstitch and French Knot, embroider facial features as indicted on graph.

3: With matching colors, Overcast unfinished edges of D pieces. Holding unworked B to wrong side of worked piece, with matching colors, Whipstitch together as indicated. Whipstitch one C to open edges of each foot as indicated; Overcast unfinished edges of feet.

NOTE: Cut string in half or separate 18" of white into 1-ply or worsted-weight into 2-ply.

4: For balloon strings, tie one end of each string or 18" length of white into a knot around each balloon; trim close. Trim opposite ends into uneven lengths as shown. Glue balloons together and to back of Boy's ear, strings to back of Boy's hand and boy to center of base as shown. Glue forget-me-knots to base over grass as shown.

GIRL
CUTTING INSTRUCTIONS:
A: For base, cut two according to Papa A graph.
B: For body, cut two according to graph.
C: For left and right arms, cut one each according to graphs.
D: For small and large foot supports, cut one 2 x 3 holes and one 3 x 3 holes (no graphs).
E: For carrots, cut two according to graph.

STITCHING INSTRUCTIONS:

1: Follow Step 1 of Papa.

2: Using colors and stitches indicated, work one B, C and E pieces according to graphs. Using colors indicated, Straight Stitch and French Knot, embroider facial features as indicated on graph. With matching colors, Overcast unfinished edges of C and E pieces.

3: Holding unworked B to wrong side of worked piece, with matching colors, Whipstitch together as indicated. Whipstitch one D to open edges of each foot as indicated; Overcast unfinished edges of dress.

NOTE: Cut one 9" length of sail blue and two 6" lengths of green.

4: Tie 9" strand of sail blue into a bow; trim ends. For carrot tops, thread one 6" strand of green through ♦ hole on each E; pull ends to even. Knot at bar and fray ends to fluff. Glue one carrot to each arm, arms and bow to Girl and Girl to center of base as shown. Glue forget-me-knots to base over grass as shown.

BABY
CUTTING INSTRUCTIONS:
NOTE: Use 10–count canvas for E.
A: For base, cut two according to Papa A graph.
B: For body, cut two according to graph.
C: For small and large foot supports, cut one 2 x 2 holes and one 2 x 3 holes (no graphs).
D: For butterfly sides, cut two according to Papa D graph.
E: For net, cut one according to graph.

COLOR KEY: Cottontail Parade

Worsted-weight	Nylon Plus™	Need-loft™	YARN AMOUNT
Fern	#57	#23	80 yds.
White	#01	#41	40 yds.
Sail Blue	#04	#35	12 yds.
Straw	#41	#19	12 yds.
Pink	#11	#07	10½ yds.
Green	#58	#28	9 yds.
Lavender	#22	#45	8 yds.
Purple	#21	#46	6 yds.
Watermelon	#54	#55	6 yds.
Orange	#17	#58	2 yds.
Black	#02	#00	1½ yds.

STITCH KEY:

— Backstitch/Straight Stitch
● French Knot
♦ Yarn Attachment (Girl)

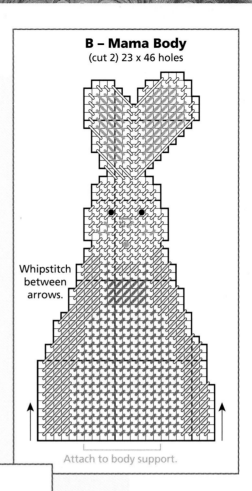

B – Mama Body
(cut 2) 23 x 46 holes

Whipstitch between arrows.

Attach to body support.

B – Papa Body
(cut 2) 25 x 43 holes

Whipstitch between arrows.

Attach to foot support.   Attach to foot support.

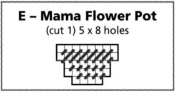

D – Butterfly Side
(cut 2) 3 x 6 holes

Whipstitch

E – Mama Flower Pot
(cut 1) 5 x 8 holes

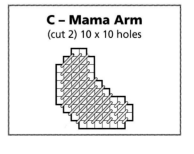

C – Mama Arm
(cut 2) 10 x 10 holes

3: Folding unworked E as indicated, with fishing line, Whipstitch together as indicated. For net handle, fold chenille stem in half. Place stem fold at top edge of net at fold line; with fishing line, Whipstitch stem to net as shown. Twist ends of stem together.

4: Holding unworked B to wrong side of worked piece with end of net handle between as indicated, with matching colors, Whipstitch together as indicated. With white, Whipstitch one C to open edges of each foot as indicated; Overcast unfinished edges of feet. Holding D pieces wrong sides together, with black, Whipstitch together as indicated, forming butterfly; with straw, Overcast unfinished edges.

5: Fold one double-headed stamen in half; glue to back of butterfly as shown. Glue butterfly to net and Baby to center of base as shown. Glue forget-me-knots to base and Baby as shown.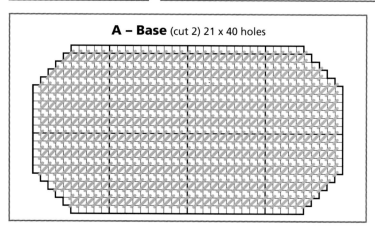

STITCHING INSTRUCTIONS:

NOTE: E piece is unworked.

1: Follow Step 1 of Papa on page 43.

2: Using colors and stitches indicated, work one B and D (one on opposite side of canvas) pieces according to graphs. Using colors indicated, Backstitch and French Knot, embroider facial features and butterfly detail as indicated on graphs.

E – Baby Net
(cut 1 from 10-count) 34 x 34 holes

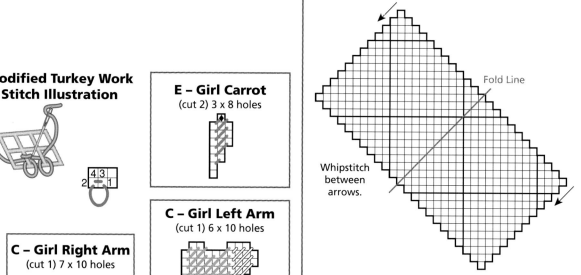

Fold Line

Whipstitch between arrows.

Modified Turkey Work Stitch Illustration

E – Girl Carrot
(cut 2) 3 x 8 holes

C – Girl Left Arm
(cut 1) 6 x 10 holes

C – Girl Right Arm
(cut 1) 7 x 10 holes

D – Boy Balloon
(cut 2) 8 x 11 holes

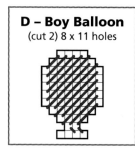

A – Base (cut 2) 21 x 40 holes

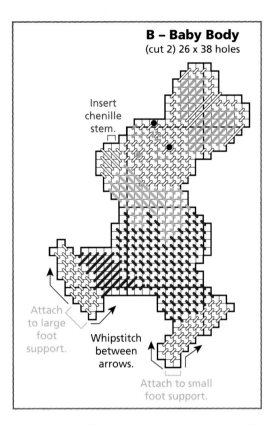

B – Baby Body
(cut 2) 26 x 38 holes

Insert chenille stem.

Attach to large foot support.

Whipstitch between arrows.

Attach to small foot support.

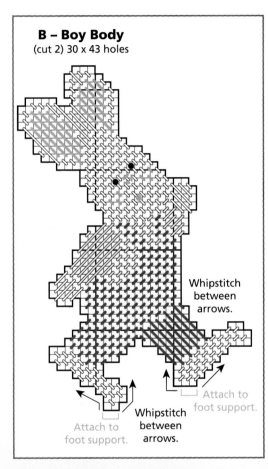

B – Boy Body
(cut 2) 30 x 43 holes

Whipstitch between arrows.

Attach to foot support.

Whipstitch between arrows.

Attach to foot support.

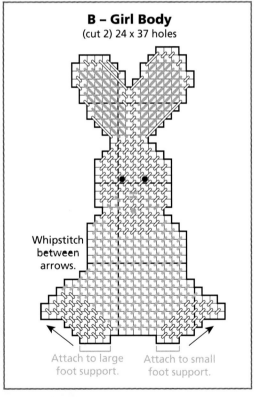

B – Girl Body
(cut 2) 24 x 37 holes

Whipstitch between arrows.

Attach to large foot support.

Attach to small foot support.

COLOR KEY: Cottontail Parade

Worsted-weight	Nylon Plus™	Need-loft™	YARN AMOUNT
Fern	#57	#23	80 yds.
White	#01	#41	40 yds.
Sail Blue	#04	#35	12 yds.
Straw	#41	#19	12 yds.
Pink	#11	#07	10½ yds.
Green	#58	#28	9 yds.
Lavender	#22	#45	8 yds.
Purple	#21	#46	6 yds.
Watermelon	#54	#55	6 yds.
Orange	#17	#58	2 yds.
Black	#02	#00	1½ yds.

STITCH KEY:

— Backstitch/Straight Stitch

● French Knot

♦ Yarn Attachment (Girl)

CELEBRATION GIFTS

SIZE: Tulip is 2¾" tall; Iris is 4¼"tall; Daffodil is 3¾" across.

MATERIALS FOR ONE OF EACH: 2½ sheets of 7-count plastic canvas; About 10 feet of heavy-gauge floral wire; Floral tape; Wire cutters; Pliers; Six-strand embroidery floss (for amounts see individual Color Keys on pages 51-52); Worsted-weight or plastic canvas yarn (for amounts see individual Color Keys).

NOTES: Graphs, diagrams and illustrations on pages 50-52. For some pieces, double plies (single plies for nylon plastic canvas yarn) of two different colors of yarn are held together for stitching; separate yarn and blend colors according to individual Color Keys. Use three strands of embroidery floss throughout; use Continental Stitch throughout.

TULIP

CUTTING INSTRUCTIONS:
A: For petals, cut six according to graph.
B: For leaves, cut two according to graph.

STITCHING INSTRUCTIONS:

1: Using colors indicated, work A and B pieces according to graphs. Fill in uncoded areas of A pieces using pink and B pieces using green.

2: To form petals and leaves, curving each piece lengthwise between thumb and finger, with matching colors, Whipstitch X edges together as indicated on graphs, pulling stitches tightly enough to hold curve; Overcast unfinished edges.

3: With right sides facing out and overlapping A pieces as indicated, with pink floss, sew three petals together (see Tulip Inner Petals Diagram). Tack edges of remaining A pieces together as indicated, forming outer petals. Place inner petals inside outer petals; sew bottoms together (see Tulip Top View Diagram).

NOTE: Cut one 2¾" length, two 3" lengths and one 17" length of wire.

4: Wrap 3" wires with floral tape. With green floss, Whipstitch one 3" wire to wrong side of seam on each leaf, allowing 1½" to extend beyond bottom.

5: Assemble Tulip according to Tulip Assembly Diagram.

By Karen Wiant

Spring Flowers

Brighten a loved one's day with a cheerful spring bouquet!

CELEBRATION GIFTS

IRIS
CUTTING INSTRUCTIONS:
   A: For inner petals, cut three according to graph.
   B: For outer petals, cut three according to graph.

STITCHING INSTRUCTIONS:

1: Using colors indicated, work A and B pieces according to graphs. Fill in uncoded areas of A pieces using lavender and B pieces using purple. With matching colors, Overcast unfinished edges. For petals, follow Step 2 of Tulip. Using yellow, Rya Knot (see Stitch Illustration) and French Knot, embroider B pieces as indicated on graph.

NOTE: Cut three 3" lengths and one 18" length of wire; wrap 3" wires and 3" on one end of 18" wire with floral tape.

2: Extending 3" wires ¾" beyond bottoms, with lavender floss, Whipstitch one wire to wrong side of dart on each B piece (see Iris Outer Petal Diagram). Alternating inner and outer petals, with right side of inner petals facing out and outer petals facing in, with floss, sew petals together as indicated.

3: With pliers, shape wrapped end of 18" wire according to Iris Stamen Diagram. With 18" wire, follow Step 3 of Tulip Assembly Diagram, continuing to wrap wire to end of stem. Bend each outer petal in an outward arc as shown in photo.

DAFFODIL
CUTTING INSTRUCTIONS:
   A: For petals, cut two according to graph.
   B: For calyx, cut one according to graph.
   C: For trumpet, cut one according to graph.
   D: For leaves, cut two according to graph.

STITCHING INSTRUCTIONS:

1: Using colors indicated, work C (overlap short ends as indicated and work through both thicknesses at overlap area to join) and D pieces according to graphs. Fill in uncoded areas of C using lemon and D using dk. green. With lemon, Whipstitch X edges of C together as indicated, pulling yarn tightly to form cup. With lemon for bottom and yellow for top, Overcast unfinished edges of trumpet.

NOTE: Cut two 5½" and one 17" length of wire; wrap wires with floral tape.

3: Using eggshell, work A pieces; Overcast unfinished edges. Using lime and fern held together, work B pieces; Whipstitch edges together and shape 17" wire according to Daffodil Calyx Diagram.

4: With green floss, Whipstitch one 5½" wire to wrong side of seam on each leaf. Holding A pieces at right angles, with eggshell, tack centers together. With yellow floss, tack bottom of trumpet to center of flower. Insert small hook on end of calyx wire into flower from bottom; sew large end of calyx to bottom of flower. Wrap stem with tape from calyx to end, attaching leaf wires as you work.

Tulip Assembly Diagram

Step 1:
Bend wires.
¾"   ¾"

1"

2¾"
wire

17"
wire

Step 2:
Wrap wires together with florist tape to secure.

Wrap

Step 3:
Slip straight end of 17" wire into center of flower and pull through bottom, forming stem; glue to secure and let dry.

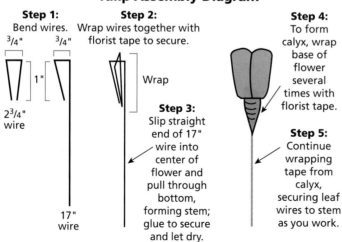

Step 4:
To form calyx, wrap base of flower several times with florist tape.

Step 5:
Continue wrapping tape from calyx, securing leaf wires to stem as you work.

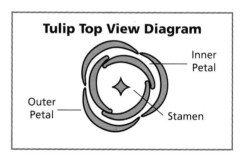

Tulip Top View Diagram

Inner Petal

Outer Petal

Stamen

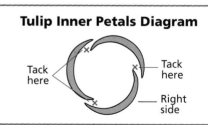

Tulip Inner Petals Diagram

Tack here

Tack here

Right side

COLOR KEY: Daffodil

Embroidery floss			AMOUNT
Green			1 yd.
Yellow			1 yd.

Worsted-weight	Nylon Plus™	Need-loft™	YARN AMOUNT
Green	#58	#28	8 yds.
Eggshell	#24	#39	8 yds.
Dk. Green	#31	#27	8 yds.
Fern	#57	#23	4 yds.
Yellow	#26	#57	3 yds.
Lemon	#25	#20	2½ yds.
Lime	#29	#22	1½ yds.

Green & Fern held together

Yellow & Lemon held together

Daffodil Calyx Diagram

Step 1:
Curl calyx between thumb and finger with right side out and Whipstitch short ends together as indicated.

¼"

1¾"

Step 2:
Whipstitch X edges together, leaving each end open.

17" wire

B – Daffodil Calyx
(cut 1) 7 x 8 holes

Whipstitch

Whipstitch

x x x x x x

Whipstitch X edges together.

C – Daffodil Trumpet
(cut 1) 9 x 23 holes

Lap under

Lap over

x x x x x x x x x x

Whipstitch X edges together.

A – Daffodil Petal
(cut 2) 19 x 20 holes

B – Tulip Leaf
(cut 2) 13 x 54 holes

Whipstitch X edges right sides together.

COLOR KEY: Tulip

Embroidery floss			AMOUNT
Green			2 yds.
Pink			1½ yds.

Worsted-weight	Nylon Plus™	Need-loft™	YARN AMOUNT
Green	#58	#28	12 yds.
Pink	#11	#07	11 yds.
Fern	#57	#23	9 yds.
Lt. Pink	#10	#08	8 yds.
Eggshell	#24	#39	2 yds.

Pink & Lt. Pink held together

Lt. Pink & Eggshell held together

Fern & Green held together

STITCH KEY:

— Overlap & Tack Inner Petals

▲ Tack Outer Petals

A – Tulip Petal
(cut 6) 11 x 17 holes

Overlap

x x

Whipstitch X edges wrong sides together.

Rya Knot
Stitch Illustration

D – Daffodil Leaf
(cut 2) 5 x 86 holes

COLOR KEY: Iris

Embroidery floss			AMOUNT
☐ Lavender			4 yds.

Worsted-weight	Nylon Plus™	Need-loft™	YARN AMOUNT
☐ Lavender	#22	#45	16 yds.
☐ Purple	#21	#46	16 yds.
☐ White	#01	#41	3 yds.
☐ Yellow	#26	#57	2 yds.
☐ Lime	#29	#22	2 yds.
■ Lime & Lavender held together			
▨ White & Purple held together			

STITCH KEY:
∽ Rya Knot
● French Knot

A – Iris Inner Petal
(cut 3) 13 x 24 holes

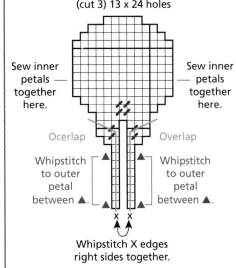

Sew inner petals together here.

Sew inner petals together here.

Ocerlap   Overlap

Whipstitch to outer petal between ▲.

Whipstitch to outer petal between ▲.

Whipstitch X edges right sides together.

B – Iris Outer Petal
(cut 3) 13 x 25 holes

Overlap   Overlap

Whipstitch to inner petal between ▲.

Whipstitch to inner petal between ▲.

Iris Stamen Diagram

Iris Outer Petal Diagram

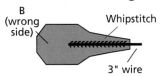

B (wrong side)

Whipstitch

3" wire

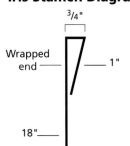

³/4"

Wrapped end

1"

18"

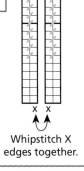

Whipstitch X edges together.

CELEBRATION GIFTS

By Carolyn Christmas

Birdhouse Wreath

Decorate a grapevine wreath with pink twisted paper, eucalyptus, Spanish moss and a happy little bird sitting outside her pretty, cozy home.

SIZE: Birdhouse is 3⅞" x 6⅞" x 6⅜" tall.

MATERIALS: Two sheets of 7-count plastic canvas; 18" grapevine wreath; Several eucalyptus sprays; 18" length of 16-gauge floral wire; Small amount of Spanish moss; Artificial bird; 3 yds. pink twisted paper; Craft glue or glue gun; Worsted-weight or plastic canvas yarn (for amounts see Color Key on page 54).

CUTTING INSTRUCTIONS: Graphs and diagram on page 54

A: For front and back, cut one each according to graph.
B: For sides, cut two 19 x 19 holes (no graph).
C: For bottom, cut one 19 x 34 holes (no graph).
D: For roof top, cut two 25 x 31 holes.
E: For roof front and back facings, cut one each according to graph.

F: For roof side facings, cut two 3 x 25 holes.
G: For roof bottom, cut two 25 x 28 holes.

STITCHING INSTRUCTIONS:

NOTE: C piece is unworked.

1: Using lt. yellow and Slanted Gobelin Stitch, work A pieces according to graph. Using pink and Slanted Gobelin Stitch over three bars, work B pieces in vertical rows. With pink, Overcast unfinished cutout edges of front A.

2: Working pink motif pattern last, using colors and stitches indicated, work D pieces according to graph. Using lt. yellow and Continental Stitch, work E and F pieces. Using lt. green and stitches indicated, work G pieces according to graph, leaving uncoded areas unworked.

3: With lt. green, Whipstitch A-C pieces together, forming house. With matching colors, Overcast unfinished edges. Holding D pieces wrong sides together,

with pink, Whipstitch together at one matching short edge. Whipstitch roof top and roof facings together according to Roof Assembly Diagram.

4: Holding G pieces wrong sides together, with lt. green, Whipstitch together at one matching short edge. With lt. yellow, Whipstitch roof bottom and roof facing together (see diagram). Glue roof to house. Wrap wreath and eucalyptus sprays with twisted paper; tie ends in bow as shown in photo.

5: Bend floral wire in half. To secure house to wreath, insert ends of wire through front opening, out through bottom of house and then through wreath; bend wire to hold. Glue bird and moss to wreath as shown. ▭

Roof Assembly Diagram

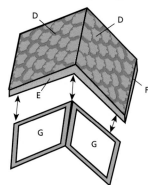

D – Roof Top (cut 2) 25 x 31 holes

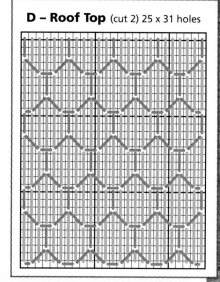

E – Roof Front & Back Facing
(cut 1 each)
31 x 31 holes

A – Front & Back
(cut 1 each) 34 x 35 holes

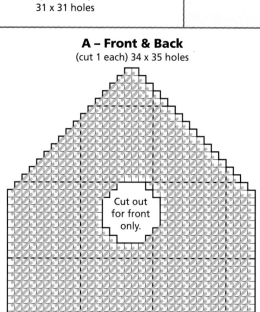

Cut out for front only.

COLOR KEY: Birdhouse Wreath

	Worsted-weight	Nylon Plus™	Need-loft™	YARN AMOUNT
	Lt. Yellow	#42	#21	36 yds.
	Lt. Green	#28	#26	20 yds.
	Pink	#11	#07	20 yds.

G – Roof Bottom
(cut 2) 25 x 28 holes

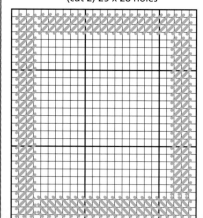

CELEBRATION GIFTS

By Michele Wilcox

Pastel Baskets

Guaranteed to brighten up the spirits, these diminutive baskets make wonderful gifts when filled with tiny treasures chosen especially for the recipient.

Pattern begins next page.

SIZE: Daisy Basket is 4¼" square x about 7" tall, including handle; Little Ducks Basket is 3" x 6¼" x about 8¼" tall, including handle.

MATERIALS: 1½ sheets of 7-count plastic canvas; Craft glue or glue gun; #3 pearl cotton or six-strand embroidery floss (for amount see Little Ducks Basket Color Key); Worsted-weight or plastic canvas yarn (for amounts see individual Color Keys).

DAISY BASKET
CUTTING INSTRUCTIONS:
   A: For sides and bottom, cut five 27 x 27 holes.
   B: For handle, cut one according to graph.

STITCHING INSTRUCTIONS:

1: Using colors and stitches indicated, work A and B pieces according to graphs. Fill in uncoded areas of B using white and Continental Stitch.

2: With matching colors, Overcast unfinished edges of handle. Holding A

pieces wrong sides together, with straw, Whipstitch together, forming basket; Overcast unfinished top edges. Glue ends of handle to basket as shown in photo.

LITTLE DUCKS BASKET
CUTTING INSTRUCTIONS:
   A: For sides, cut two according to graph.
   B: For ends, cut two according to graph.
   C: For bottom, cut one 9 x 33 holes (no graph).
   D: For handle, cut one according to graph.

STITCHING INSTRUCTIONS:

1: Using colors indicated and Continental Stitch, work A, B and D pieces according to graphs. Fill in uncoded areas of A and B pieces and work C using white and Continental Stitch. Using pearl cotton or six strands floss and French Knot, embroider eyes as indicated on graph.

2: Holding A and B pieces wrong sides together, with white, Whipstitch side edges together as indicated. Whipstitch sides, ends and C together, forming basket. Overcast unfinished edges of basket and handle. Glue ends of handle to basket as shown in photo.

B – Daisy Basket Handle
(cut 1)
17 x 90 holes

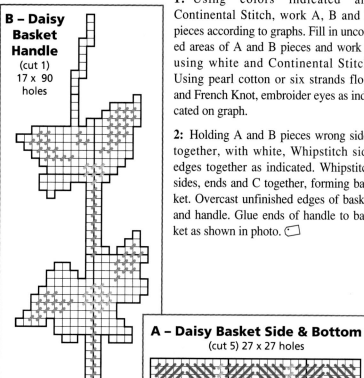

A – Daisy Basket Side & Bottom
(cut 5) 27 x 27 holes

COLOR KEY: Daisy Basket

Worsted-weight	Nylon Plus™	Needloft™	YARN AMOUNT
Lavender	#22	#45	54 yds.
Straw	#41	#19	30 yds.
Dk. Green	#31	#27	10 yds.
White	#01	#41	5 yds.

COLOR KEY: Little Ducks Basket

#3 pearl cotton or floss			AMOUNT
■ Black			½ yd.

Worsted-weight	Nylon Plus™	Need-loft™	YARN AMOUNT
☐ White	#01	#41	50 yds.
◩ Straw	#41	#19	25 yds.
▨ Dk. Green	#31	#27	18 yds.
▨ Dusty Rose	#52	#06	10 yds.
▨ Pumpkin	#50	#12	1½ yds.

STITCH KEY:

● French Knot

B – Little Ducks Basket End
(cut 2) 19 x 26 holes

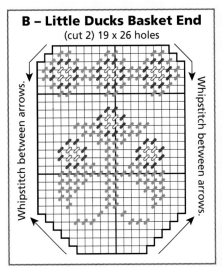

Whipstitch between arrows. (left side)

Whipstitch between arrows. (right side)

A – Little Ducks Basket Side
(cut 2) 26 x 43 holes

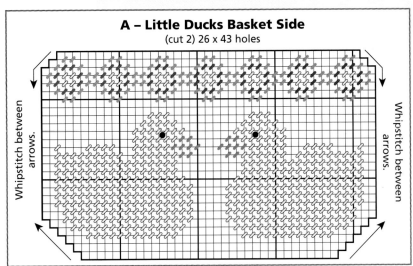

Whipstitch between arrows. (left side)

Whipstitch between arrows. (right side)

D – Little Ducks Basket Handle
(cut 1) 7 x 85 holes

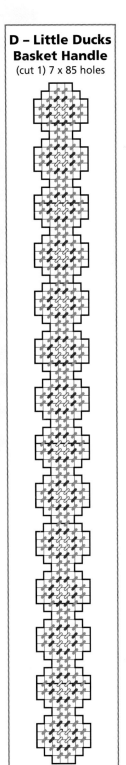

WEDDING BELLS

CELEBRATION GIFTS

SIZE: Stands 9" tall.

MATERIALS: Two sheets of 7-count plastic canvas; Eleven small white silk roses; Small amount of floral tape; ⅞ yd. white 1" gathered lace; 8" square scrap of white tulle; 1 yd. each of several different colors of ⅛" satin ribbons; One package chenille stems in desired hair color; Craft glue or glue gun; Worsted-weight or plastic canvas yarn (for amounts see Color Key on page 63).

CUTTING INSTRUCTIONS: Graphs and diagrams on pages 62-63.

A: For bride and groom heads, cut one each according to graph.
B: For bride arms, cut one according to graph.
C: For groom hands, cut two according to graph.
D: For bride skirt, cut one according to graph.
E: For bride bodice, cut one according to graph.
F: For groom shirt, cut one according to graph.
G: For groom jacket front, cut two according to graph.
H: For groom jacket back, cut two according to graph.
I: For groom left sleeve, cut one according to graph.
J: For groom right sleeve, cut one according to graph.
K: For groom pants, cut two according to graph.
L: For groom bow tie, cut one according to graph.

STITCHING INSTRUCTIONS:

NOTE: Use Continental Stitch throughout.

1: For bride head and arms and groom head and hands, with lt. pink, work A, B and C pieces.

2: For bride skirt, bodice and groom shirt, with white, work D (overlapping 7 holes as indicated on graph and working through both thicknesses at overlap area to join), E and F pieces.

3: For groom jacket and pants, with black, work G (one on opposite side of canvas), H (one on opposite side of canvas; overlap pieces as indicated and according to Groom Jacket Back Assembly Diagram and work through both thicknesses at overlap area to join), I, J and K pieces.

BRIDE ASSEMBLY:

1: Overlapping two holes on A piece as indicated and holding wrong sides together, with lt. pink, Whipstitch X edges together as indicated, stuffing with fiberfill before closing. Tack A to E as indicated on E graph.

2: For shoulders, holding E pieces wrong sides together, with white, Whipstitch X edges together as indicated. Starting at waist, Whipstitch side seams as indicated, leaving waist open. Overcast waist and armhole edge of E, then waist and bottom edge of D. Fill E with fiberfill through waist opening.

3: Glue E to inside of D at waist. Glue B to armhole edges of E.

NOTES: For veil, cut 8" circle from tulle. Cut stems off two small roses. For bouquet, trim nine small rose stems to 4" each.

4: For hair, glue chenille to head (see Bride Hair Assembly Diagram). Gather veil at one point 1" from edge and glue to bangs as shown in photo; glue two roses to veil as shown. Glue lace to E as indicated on graph.

5: Wrap floral tape around rose stems to form bouquet. Tie ribbon centers around stems and twist stems around bride's hands. Tie free ends of ribbons together in knot about 6" from ends. Leave ribbon hanging for later use.

GROOM ASSEMBLY:

1: Substituting F for E, follow Steps 1 and 2 of Bride Assembly.

2: Holding one K piece wrong sides together, with black, Whipstitch leg seams as indicated and according to Groom Pants Assembly Diagram. Repeat for remaining K piece. To form pants, Whipstitch front and back seams as indicated. (It is not necessary to Whipstitch from front to back seam, as it will not show.) Overcast waist and bottom edges of K pieces. Glue F to inside of K at waist.

3: Holding wrong sides together, with black, Whipstitch G and H pieces together as indicated.

4: With black and easing to fit, Whipstitch G and H to I and J pieces at armhole edges (be careful to have right and left sleeves on correct sides). Holding wrong sides together, Whipstitch X edges together on I piece as indicated. Holding wrong sides together, Whipstitch underarm seams on J and I pieces. Overcast unfinished edges of jacket and L piece.

5: For lapels, fold jacket front as indicated on G graph. Tack lapels to jacket to secure. Glue C pieces to inside of cuffs.

CELEBRATION GIFTS

By Sandra Miller-Maxfield

Bride & Groom

All dressed up for a day to remember, this promising couple can be made in wedding colors to decorate a table for a shower or reception.

6: For hair, glue chenille to head (see Groom Hair Assembly Diagram). Glue gathered lace to shirt as shown in photo. Glue L to lace under chin.

FINISHING

Glue groom's right leg to bride's skirt matching hems (excluding lace). Glue groom's right arm behind bride with his hand slightly below her waist on right side. Glue ribbon knot behind groom's left hand, leaving streamer ends free.

C – Groom Hand
(cut 2) 4 x 8 holes

L – Bow Tie
(cut 1) 4 x 4 holes

B – Bride Arms (cut 1) 12 x 27 holes

E – Bride Bodice
(cut 1) 16 x 30 holes

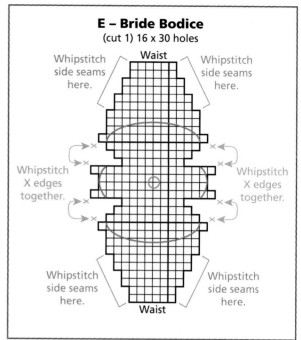

Waist

Whipstitch side seams here.

Whipstitch side seams here.

Whipstitch X edges together.

Whipstitch X edges together.

Whipstitch side seams here.

Whipstitch side seams here.

Waist

Groom Hair Assembly Diagram

1. Front   2. Side   3. Back

Jacket Back Assembly Diagram

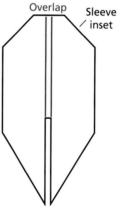

Overlap   Sleeve inset

Bride Hair Assembly Diagram

1. Front   2. Back   3. Front

Glue Veil Here

K – Pants
(cut 2) 16 x 34 holes

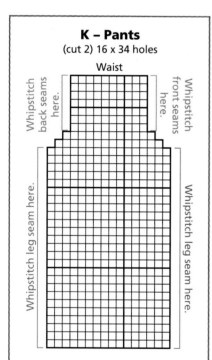

Waist

Whipstitch back seams here.

Whipstitch front seams here.

Whipstitch leg seam here.

Whipstitch leg seam here.

G – Jacket Front
(cut 2) 9 x 24 holes

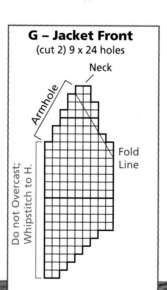

Neck

Armhole

Fold Line

Do not Overcast; Whipstitch to H.

F – Groom Shirt
(cut 1) 16 x 31 holes

Waist

Whipstitch side seams here.

Whipstitch side seams here.

Whipstitch X edges together.

Whipstitch X edges together.

Whipstitch side seams here.

Whipstitch side seams here.

Waist

COLOR KEY: Bride & Groom

Worsted-weight	Nylon Plus™	Need-loft™	YARN AMOUNT
☐ White	#01	#41	42 yds.
☐ Black	#02	#00	32 yds.
☐ Lt. Pink	#10	#08	12 yds.

STITCH KEY:

○ Head Attachment

❤ Bouquet Placement

— Lace Attachment

Pants Assembly Diagram

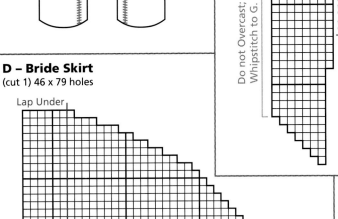

H – Jacket Back
(cut 2) 8 x 32 holes

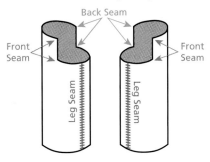

A – Bride & Groom Head
(cut 1 each) 10 x 16 holes

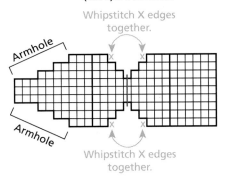

I – Groom Left Sleeve
(cut 1) 9 x 26 holes

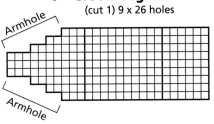

J – Groom Right Sleeve
(cut 1) 9 x 26 holes

D – Bride Skirt
(cut 1) 46 x 79 holes

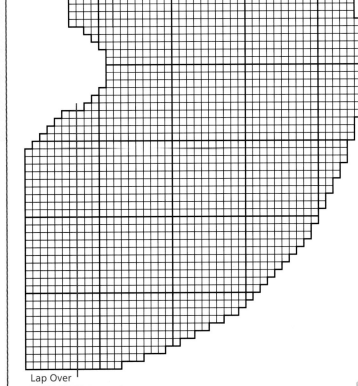

CELEBRATION GIFTS

By Trudy Bath Smith

Sweetheart Keepsakes

Keep mementos of a wedding day close at hand and beautifully displayed in this heart-trimmed photo album, trinket box and invitation frame.

PHOTO ALBUM

SIZE: 2½" x 12" x 12"; covers a 2" spine, 3-ring binder. Front holds a 3½" x 4½" photo.

MATERIALS: Four sheets of 12" x 18" or larger 7-count plastic canvas; 2" spine, 3-ring binder; 12" x 12" white felt; Craft glue or glue gun; Metallic cord (for amounts see Color Key on page 67); Worsted-weight or plastic canvas yarn (for amount see Color Key).

CUTTING INSTRUCTIONS: Graphs on pages 67-68.

A: For front, cut one according to graph.
B: For back, cut one 79 x 79 holes (no graph).
C: For spine, cut one 16 x 79 holes (no graph).
D: For heart, cut one according to graph.
E: For heart lining, cut one 33 x 39 holes (no graph).
F: For notched and square flaps, cut one according to graph and one 70 x 79 holes (no graph).

STITCHING INSTRUCTIONS:

NOTE: E and F pieces are unworked.

1: Using colors and stitches indicated, work A according to graph. Fill in uncoded areas using white and Continental Stitch. Using white and Slanted Gobelin Stitch over three bars, work B and C pieces in vertical rows. Using white/pink cord and Continental Stitch, work D according to graph, leaving uncoded areas unworked.

2: With white/silver cord, Overcast unfinished cutout edges of A and D. Holding unworked E to wrong side of D, with white/pink cord, Whipstitch side and bottom edges together as indicated on graph. Glue right side of heart to wrong side of A over cutout.

3: Holding unworked notched F to

wrong side of front with notch at top and matching outer edges as indicated, with white, Whipstitch straight edges together (**NOTE:** Notched edges of flap are unfinished.); Overcast unfinished top edge of front. Holding remaining unworked F to wrong side of back and matching outer edges, Whipstitch together.

4: Holding front and back wrong sides together with spine between, Whipstitch together; Overcast remaining unfinished edges. Glue felt to front of binder. Slip binder into flaps. Insert photo through top of cover and between heart and lining.

FRAME
SIZE: 7" x 12½"; holds two 4½" x 5½" photos.

MATERIALS: One sheet of 7-count plastic canvas; One sheet of white 7-count plastic canvas; 9" x 12" poster board or cardboard; Metallic cord (for amounts see Color Key on page 66); Worsted-weight or plastic canvas yarn (for amount see Color Key).

CUTTING INSTRUCTIONS: Graph on page 66.
NOTE: Use white canvas for backs.
A: For fronts and backs, cut two each according to graph.
B: For photo backing, using one back A as pattern, cut two from poster board ⅛" smaller at all edges.

STITCHING INSTRUCTIONS:

NOTE: Back A pieces are unworked.

1: Using colors and stitches indicated, work front A pieces according to graph. Fill in uncoded areas using white and Continental Stitch. With white/silver cord, Overcast unfinished cutout edges.

2: For each side, holding one back A

4: Slide B pieces into frames.

TREASURE BOX

SIZE: 4" x 4⅜" x 2¼" tall.

MATERIALS: One sheet of 7-count plastic canvas; One sheet of white 7-count plastic canvas; Metallic cord (for amounts see color Key); Worsted-weight or plastic canvas yarn (for amount see Color Key).

CUTTING INSTRUCTIONS:
NOTE: Use white canvas for lining pieces.
A: For lid top and lining, cut one of each color 26 x 28 holes.

to wrong side of one front, with white, Whipstitch one side and bottom edges together as indicated on graph.

3: Holding sides right sides together and working through all thicknesses, with white, Whipstitch together at matching unfinished straight edges. Whipstitch remaining unfinished corner edges together, leaving top straight edges unjoined. Overcast top edges of each front.

COLOR KEY: Frame

Metallic cord			AMOUNT
White/Silver			16 yds.
Pink/Silver			8 yds.

Worsted-weight	Nylon Plus™	Need-loft™	YARN AMOUNT
White	#01	#41	82 yds.

COLOR KEY: Treasure Box

Metallic cord			AMOUNT
White/Silver			3 yds.
Pink/Silver			2 yds.

Worsted-weight	Nylon Plus™	Need-loft™	YARN AMOUNT
White	#01	#41	84 yds.

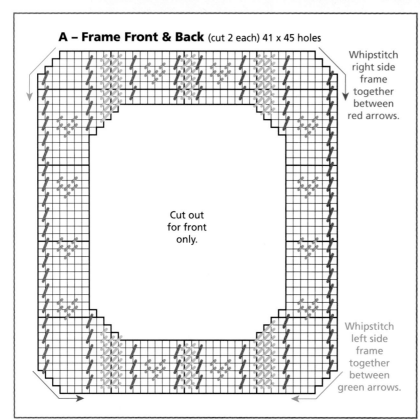

A – Frame Front & Back (cut 2 each) 41 x 45 holes

Whipstitch right side frame together between red arrows.

Cut out for front only.

Whipstitch left side frame together between green arrows.

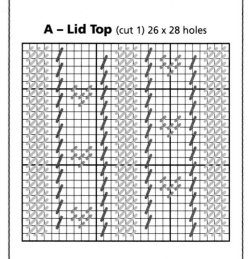

A – Lid Top (cut 1) 26 x 28 holes

A – Photo Album Front (cut 1) 79 x 79 holes

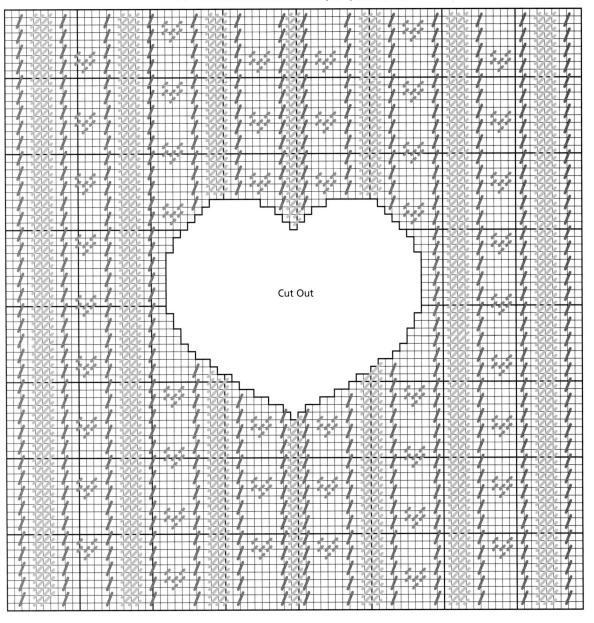

Cut Out

D – Photo Album Heart (cut 1) 33 x 39 holes

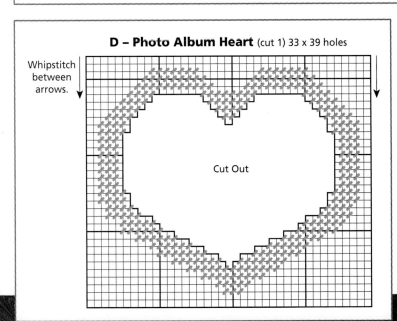

Whipstitch between arrows.

Cut Out

COLOR KEY: Photo Album

Metallic cord			AMOUNT
White/Silver			40 yds.
Pink/Silver			27 yds.

Worsted-weight	Nylon Plus™	Need-loft™	YARN AMOUNT
White	#01	#41	4¹/₂ oz.

B: For lid sides and linings, cut two of each color 4 x 26 holes and two of each color 4 x 28 holes (no graphs).

C: For box sides and linings, cut two of each color 12 x 24 holes and two of each color 12 x 26 holes (no graphs).
D: For box bottom, cut one of each color 24 x 26 holes (no graphs).

STITCHING INSTRUCTIONS:

NOTE: Lining and D pieces are unworked.

1: Using colors and stitches indicated, work A according to graph. Fill in uncoded areas using white and Continental Stitch. Using white and Slanted Gobelin Stitch over narrow width for lid sides and Continental Stitch for box sides, work B and C pieces.

2: Holding lining pieces to wrong side of worked pieces and working through all thicknesses at matching edges, with white, Whipstitch A and B pieces together, forming lid; Whipstitch C and D pieces together, forming box.

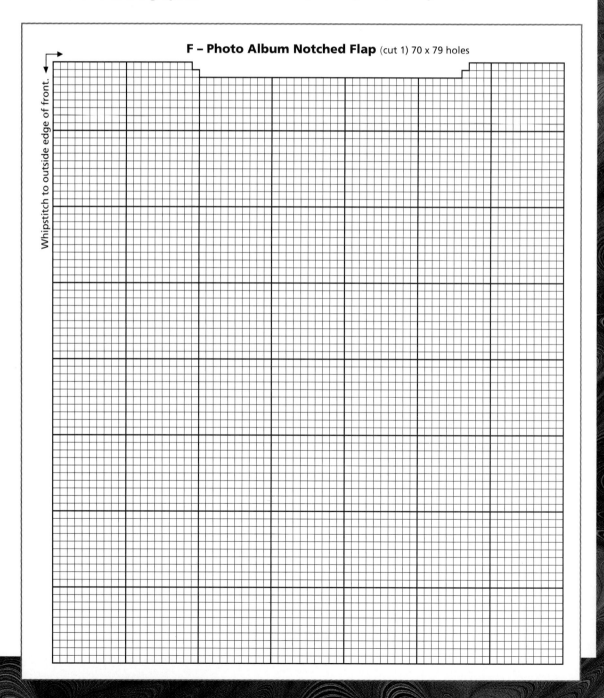

F – Photo Album Notched Flap (cut 1) 70 x 79 holes

Whipstitch to outside edge of front.

CELEBRATION GIFTS

By Carolyn Christmas

Gift Wrap Box

Add a personal touch to any gift-giving occasion with this fanciful striped gift box topped with a perky bow. It's great for storing photos or other keepsakes, too.

SIZE: 8½" across x 8⅜" tall.

MATERIALS: Six sheets of 7-count plastic canvas; Craft glue or glue gun; Worsted-weight or plastic canvas yarn (for amounts see Color Key).

CUTTING INSTRUCTIONS:
A: For box sides and linings, cut twelve 25 x 53 holes (no graph).
B: For box bottom, cut one according to graph.
C: For lid sides, cut six 12 x 27 holes.
D: For lid top, cut one according to graph.
E: For bow loops, cut one according to graph.

F: For knot, cut one 6 x 21 holes (no graph).
G: For tails, cut one according to graph.

STITCHING INSTRUCTIONS:

NOTE: Lining A pieces and B are unworked.

1: Using colors and stitches indicated, work six A pieces according to Box Side Stitch Pattern Guide, and work C, D, E (overlap three holes at ends and work through all thicknesses at center to join as indicated on graph) and G pieces according to graphs. Using burgundy and Slanted Gobelin Stitch over narrow width, work F.

2: Holding lining A pieces to wrong side of worked pieces and working through all thicknesses, with burgundy, Whipstitch A and B pieces together, forming box; Whipstitch unfinished edges together. Whipstitch C and D pieces together, forming lid; Overcast unfinished edges.

3: Overcast unfinished edges of E, G and long edges of F. Wrapping short ends of F wrong sides together around center of bow loops, Whipstitch together, forming bow. Glue bow and tails to lid as shown in photo.

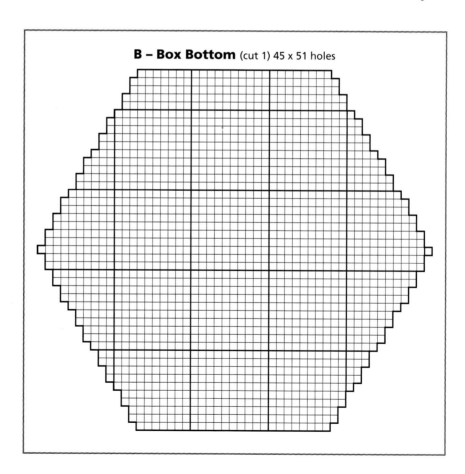

B – Box Bottom (cut 1) 45 x 51 holes

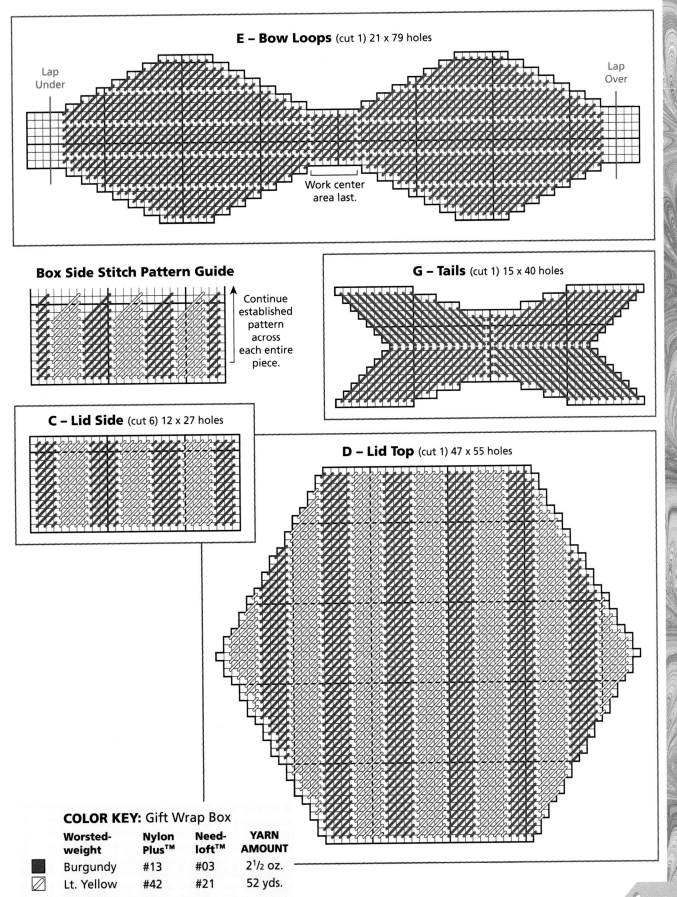

E – Bow Loops (cut 1) 21 x 79 holes

Lap Under

Lap Over

Work center area last.

Box Side Stitch Pattern Guide

Continue established pattern across each entire piece.

G – Tails (cut 1) 15 x 40 holes

C – Lid Side (cut 6) 12 x 27 holes

D – Lid Top (cut 1) 47 x 55 holes

COLOR KEY: Gift Wrap Box

	Worsted-weight	Nylon Plus™	Need-loft™	YARN AMOUNT
■	Burgundy	#13	#03	2½ oz.
◪	Lt. Yellow	#42	#21	52 yds.

CELEBRATION GIFTS

For an unforgettable wedding present, enclose your gift in this splendidly decorated two-tiered wedding cake complete with bride and groom.

CELEBRATION GIFTS

By Renee Stewart

Wedding Cake

SIZE: 9⅜" across x 15½" tall.

MATERIALS: Six sheets of 7-count plastic canvas; Four 9½" plastic canvas circles; 4" bride and groom; Five white ¾" white doves; One white 2" bell; Two gold ¾" rings; One 11½" x 14" piece of white poster board; Six white 2½" silk roses; Eighteen small white silk flower sprays; Twenty-six white 1" silk flowers; Craft glue or glue gun; Worsted-weight or plastic canvas yarn (for amount see Color Key on page 74).

CUTTING INSTRUCTIONS: Graphs and diagram on page 74.

A: For large cake box sides, cut two 30 x 63 holes and one 30 x 61 holes (no graphs).
B: For large cake box side lining, cut two 29 x 60 holes and one 29 x 62 holes (no graphs).
C: For small cake box sides, cut two 29 x 67 holes (no graph).
D: For reinforcements, cut three 5 x 30 holes and five 5 x 29 holes (no graphs).
E: For large cake box bottom, from one canvas circle, trim off one outside row of holes (no graph).
F: For large cake box bottom lining, from one canvas circle, trim off two outside rows of holes (no graph).
G: For large lid, use one canvas circle (no graph).
H: For large lid lip pieces, cut two according to #1 and one according to #2 graphs.
I: For large lid lip reinforcements, cut three according to graph.
J: For small lid, from one canvas circle, trim off nine outside rows of holes (no graph).
K: For small lid lip pieces, cut two according to #1 and one according to #2 graphs.
L: For small lid lip reinforcements, cut three according to graph.
M: For gazebo front and back, cut one each according to graph.
N: For gazebo sides, cut two according to graph.
O: For gazebo roof, cut two 15 x 20 holes (no graph).

P: For large box bottom lining, using F as a pattern, cut one from poster board ⅛" smaller at all edges.

STITCHING INSTRUCTIONS:

NOTE: B, E and F pieces are unworked.

1: Using white and Slanted Gobelin Stitch over two bars, work A pieces in vertical rows, joining one large D piece between short ends of each A as you work (see Reinforcement Diagram), forming side. Repeat with C pieces and two small D pieces. Overcast one unfinished edge of small box.

2: For large box side lining, Whipstitch short ends of B pieces together using remaining small D pieces as in Step 1.

3: Using white and Slanted Gobelin Stitch over two bars, work J piece from center out and eleven outside rows of G. Using white and Continental Stitch, work H and I pieces together as in Step 1. Repeat with K and L pieces. Holding wrong sides together, Whipstitch G and H pieces together, forming large lid. Overcast unfinished edges. Repeat with J and K pieces.

4: Whipstitch and assemble pieces according to Cake Assembly Diagram.

5: Using stitches indicated, work M and N pieces according to graphs. Using Continental Stitch, work O pieces. Holding wrong sides together, Whipstitch M, N and O pieces together, forming gazebo. Overcast unfinished roof edges of M pieces as indicated on graph. Sew bell to wrong side at center top of roof.

6: Glue gazebo to center of small box lid and bride and groom in center of gazebo as shown in photo. Glue doves to roof and flowers to scallops on boxes as shown.

Reinforcement Diagram

Center hole of reinforcement piece is to be used as part of stitch pattern.

Overlap two holes on each side of reinforcement piece. Stitch pattern through all thicknesses.

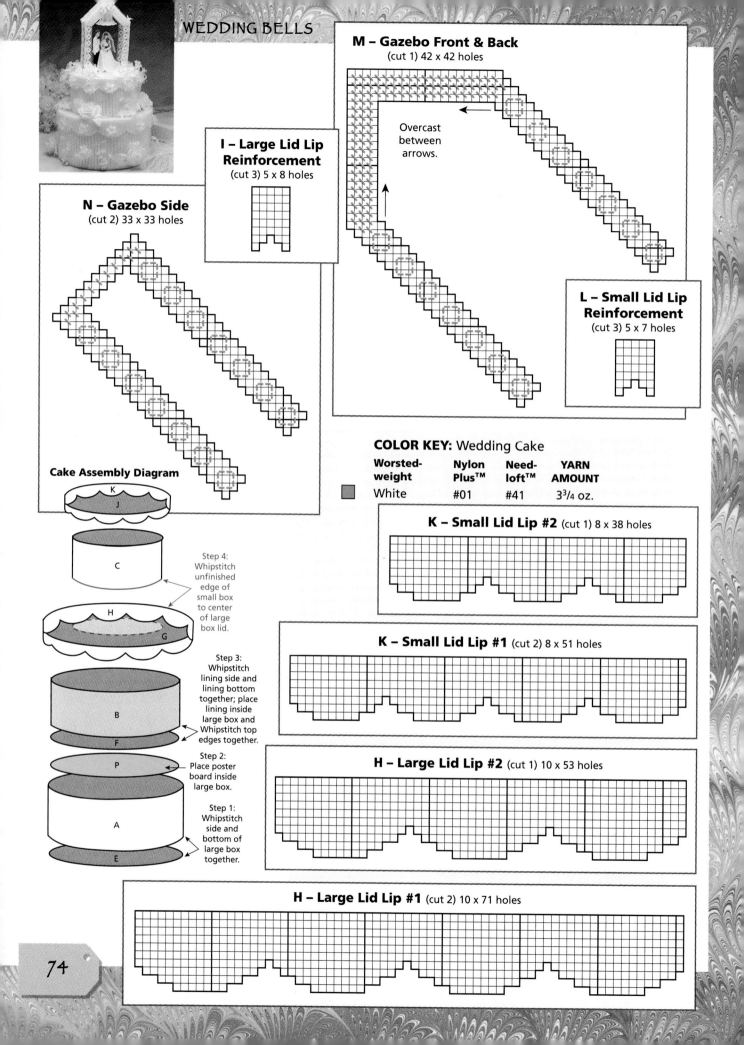

M – Gazebo Front & Back
(cut 1) 42 x 42 holes

Overcast between arrows.

I – Large Lid Lip Reinforcement
(cut 3) 5 x 8 holes

N – Gazebo Side
(cut 2) 33 x 33 holes

L – Small Lid Lip Reinforcement
(cut 3) 5 x 7 holes

Cake Assembly Diagram

COLOR KEY: Wedding Cake

Worsted-weight	Nylon Plus™	Need-loft™	YARN AMOUNT
White	#01	#41	3³/4 oz.

K – Small Lid Lip #2 (cut 1) 8 x 38 holes

K – Small Lid Lip #1 (cut 2) 8 x 51 holes

Step 4: Whipstitch unfinished edge of small box to center of large box lid.

Step 3: Whipstitch lining side and lining bottom together; place lining inside large box and Whipstitch top edges together.

Step 2: Place poster board inside large box.

Step 1: Whipstitch side and bottom of large box together.

H – Large Lid Lip #2 (cut 1) 10 x 53 holes

H – Large Lid Lip #1 (cut 2) 10 x 71 holes

CELEBRATION GIFTS

LIBERTY

By Trudy Bath Smith

**Strike up the band!
Show your patriotic spirit with
this nine-piece celebration set
stitched in red, white and blue
and highlighted with gold
braid and stars.**

Independence Day

CELEBRATION GIFTS

COASTERS

SIZE: Each Coaster is 3⅛" x 3½"; Holder is 2⅜" x 3⅞" x 1¼" tall.

MATERIALS: One sheet of 7-count plastic canvas; Heavy metallic braid or metallic cord (for amount see Color Key on page 79); Worsted-weight or plastic canvas yarn (for amounts see Color Key).

CUTTING INSTRUCTIONS: Graphs on page 79.
A: For Coasters, cut four according to graph.
B: For Holder front and back, cut one each 15 x 24 holes.
C: For Holder sides, cut two 7 x 15 holes.
D: For Holder bottom, cut one 7 x 25 holes (no graph).

STITCHING INSTRUCTIONS:

NOTE: D piece is unworked.

1: Using colors and stitches indicated, work A-C pieces according to graphs. Using metallic braid or cord and Backstitch, embroider coasters as indicated on A graph. With matching colors, Overcast unfinished edges of Coasters.

2: With matching colors, Whipstitch B-D pieces together; with metallic braid or cord, Overcast unfinished edges of Holder.

TRINKET HAT

SIZE: 2¾" x 4¾".

MATERIALS: ½ sheet of 7-count plastic canvas; Three 4½" plastic canvas radial circles; Six gold ⅝" star sequins; Six gold 3-mm. pearl beads; Worsted-weight or plastic canvas yarn (for amounts see Color Key on page 78).

CUTTING INSTRUCTIONS: Graphs and illustration on pages 78-79.
A: For side, cut one 15 x 60 holes (no graph).
B: For brim, cut one from 4½" circle according to graph.
C: For top, cut one from 4½" circle according to graph.
D: For lid top, use one 4½" circle.
E: For lid brim, cut one 4½" circle according to graph.
F: For lid lip pieces, cut two 2 x 49 holes (no graph).

STITCHING INSTRUCTIONS:

1: Using colors and stitches indicated, work A according to Hat Side Stitch Pattern Guide; work B-E

pieces according to graphs. Overlapping two holes at each short end and working through both thicknesses at overlap areas to join, using royal and Continental Stitch, work F pieces. With matching colors, Whipstitch short ends of A together.

2: Whipstitch A-C pieces together; Overcast unfinished edge. Holding D to wrong side of E, Whipstitch together at inside cutout edge. Whipstitch F to D, forming lip; Overcast unfinished edge.

3: Sew stars and sequins around hat side as shown in photo.

EAGLE TISSUE COVER

SIZE: Snugly covers a boutique-style tissue box.

MATERIALS: Two sheets of 7-count plastic canvas; 20 gold ⅝" star sequins, 20 gold 3-mm. pearl beads; Sewing needle and matching color thread; Worsted-weight or plastic canvas yarn (for amounts see Color Key on page 80).

CUTTING INSTRUCTIONS: Graphs on pages 80-81.
A: For front, cut one according to graph.
B: For sides and back, cut three 29 x 37 holes.
C: For top, cut one according to graph.
D: For wing back, cut one according to graph.
E: For tail back, cut one according to graph.

STITCHING INSTRUCTIONS:

1: Using colors and stitches indicated, work A-E pieces according to graphs; with royal, Overcast unfinished cutout edges of C.

2: With matching colors, Whipstitch A-C pieces together; Overcast bottom edges of cover. Holding matching wing and tail back pieces to wrong side of extensions on front, with maple, Whipstitch D and E pieces to A.

3: Sew stars and sequins to cover as shown in photo.

UNCLE SAM

SIZE: 7⅜" tall.

MATERIALS: One sheet of 7-count plastic canvas; 16 gold 3-mm. pearl beads; One white 6" beverage stir stick; Sewing needle and matching color thread; Craft glue or glue gun; Heavy metallic braid or

3: For hat, Whipstitch E-H pieces together according to Uncle Sam Hat Assembly Diagram; with royal, Overcast unfinished edges. Glue a strand of braid or cord around hat as shown in photo.

4: For flag, sew beads to I pieces as indicated. Holding I pieces wrong sides together, with matching colors, Whipstitch together. With red, sew flag to stir stick as shown. Glue stick between hands as shown.

LIBERTY WREATH

SIZE: 14" across.

MATERIALS: Two sheets of 7-count plastic canvas; Six gold ⅝" star sequins; Six gold 3-mm. pearl beads; 14" Styrofoam® wreath; 12 yds. blue 1⅜" craft ribbon; Sewing needle and matching color thread; Straight pins; Craft glue or glue gun; Heavy metallic braid or metallic cord (for amount see Color Key on page 81); Worsted-weight or plastic canvas yarn (for amounts see Color Key).

CUTTING INSTRUCTIONS: Graphs on page 81.
   A: For eagle, cut one according to graph.
   B: For banner, cut one according to graph.
   C: For tail pieces, cut one each according to graphs.

STITCHING INSTRUCTIONS:

1: Overlapping banner and tail pieces as indicated on graphs and working through both thicknesses at overlap areas to join, using colors and stitches indicated, work A-C pieces according to graphs; with red for banner and with matching colors, Overcast unfinished edges.

2: Using black for eye and metallic braid or cord for shield detail and Straight Stitch, embroider as indicated on graph.

NOTE: Cut two 12" lengths of ribbon; set aside.

3: Covering completely, wrap wreath with ribbon, securing with pins as needed. Glue eagle to wreath as shown in photo. Glue one end of each 12" ribbon to back of eagle; bring opposite ends over front of wreath and secure with pins at back.

4: Sew beads and stars to ribbon and glue banner to wreath as shown. ▱

metallic cord (for amount see Color Key on page 80); Worsted-weight or plastic canvas yarn (for amounts see Color Key).

CUTTING INSTRUCTIONS: Graphs and diagram on pages 80-81.
   A: For body, cut two according to graph.
   B: For arms, cut four according to graph.
   C: For legs, cut four according to graph.
   D: For soles, cut two according to graph.
   E: For hat sides, cut two 9 x 11 holes.
   F: For hat top, cut one 1 x 11 holes (no graph).
   G: For hat ends, cut two 1 x 9 holes (no graph).
   H: For hat brim, cut one according to graph.
   I: For flag, cut two according to graph.

STITCHING INSTRUCTIONS:

1: Using colors and stitches indicated, work A-E (one A and two each B and C pieces on opposite side of canvas), H and I (one on opposite side of canvas) pieces according to graphs. Using black and French Knot for eyes and metallic braid or cord and Backstitch for jacket detail, embroider as indicated on A and B graphs.

2: For body, holding A pieces wrong sides together, with matching colors, Whipstitch together. Repeat for arms and legs, leaving bottom edges of legs unjoined as indicated. With black, Whipstitch one D to bottom edges of each leg. With matching colors, tack arms and legs to body as indicated.

Hat Side Stitch Pattern Guide

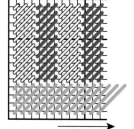

Continue established pattern across entire piece.

COLOR KEY: Trinket Hat

Worsted-weight	Nylon Plus™	Need-loft™	YARN AMOUNT
▨ Royal	#09	#32	18 yds.
▰ Red	#19	#02	10 yds.
▨ White	#01	#41	10 yds.

COLOR KEY: Coasters & Holder

Heavy metallic braid or cord			AMOUNT
Gold			6 yds.

Worsted-weight	Nylon Plus™	Need-loft™	YARN AMOUNT
Red	#19	#02	18 yds.
Royal	#09	#32	18 yds.
White	#01	#41	18 yds.

STITCH KEY:

— Backstitch/Straight Stitch

A – Coaster
(cut 4) 20 x 23 holes

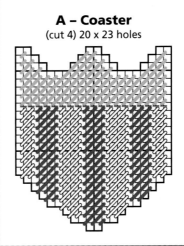

B – Holder Front & Back
(cut 1 each) 15 x 24 holes

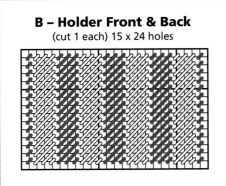

D – Trinket Hat Lid Top
(use 4$^1/_2$" circle)

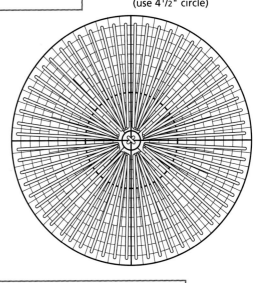

C – Holder Side
(cut 2)
7 x 15 holes

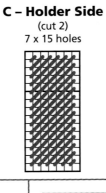

B – Trinket Hat Brim
(cut 1 from 4$^1/_2$" circle)
Cut away gray areas.

C – Trinket Hat Top
(cut 1 from 4$^1/_2$" circle)

E – Trinket Hat Lid Brim
(cut 1 from 4$^1/_2$" circle)
Cut away gray area.

A – Tissue Cover Front
(cut 1) 35 x 37 holes

B – Tissue Cover Side & Back
(cut 3) 29 x 37 holes

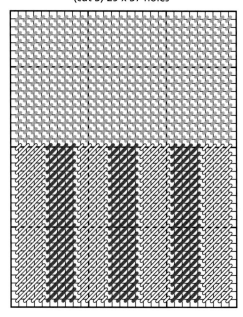

C – Tissue Cover Top
(cut 1) 29 x 29 holes

Cut Out

H – Uncle Sam Hat Brim
(cut 1)
6 x 15 holes

Cut Out

E – Uncle Sam Hat Side
(cut 2)
9 x 11 holes

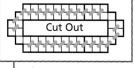

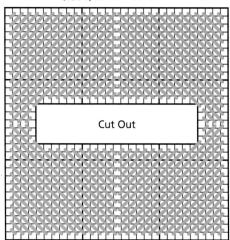

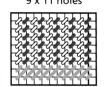

COLOR KEY: Tissue Cover

	Worsted-weight	Nylon Plus™	Need-loft™	YARN AMOUNT
	Royal	#09	#32	25 yds.
	Red	#19	#02	13 yds.
	White	#01	#41	13 yds.
	Maple	#35	#13	10 yds.
	Gold	#27	#17	2 yds.
	Black	#02	#00	1 yd.

COLOR KEY: Uncle Sam

	Heavy metallic braid or cord			AMOUNT
	Gold			5 yds.

	Worsted-weight	Nylon Plus™	Need-loft™	YARN AMOUNT
	Royal	#09	#32	15 yds.
	White	#01	#41	10 yds.
	Red	#19	#02	7 yds.
	Black	#02	#00	5 yds.
	Flesh	#14	#56	2 yds.

STITCH KEY:

— Backstitch/Straight Stitch
♦ Arm/Leg Attachment
○ Bead Star Attachment

Uncle Sam Hat Assembly Diagram

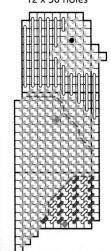

A – Uncle Sam Body
(cut 2)
12 x 30 holes

C – Uncle Sam Leg
(cut 4)
11 x 16 holes

Whipstitch between arrows.

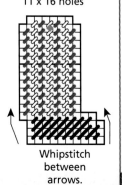

B – Uncle Sam Arm
(cut 4)
4 x 16 holes

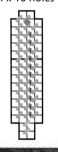

I – Uncle Sam Flag
(cut 2)
11 x 14 holes

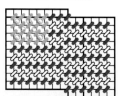

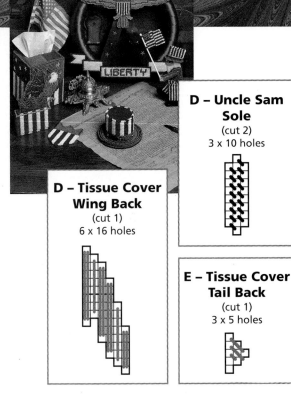

D – Uncle Sam Sole
(cut 2)
3 x 10 holes

D – Tissue Cover Wing Back
(cut 1)
6 x 16 holes

E – Tissue Cover Tail Back
(cut 1)
3 x 5 holes

COLOR KEY: Liberty Wreath

Heavy metallic braid or cord			AMOUNT
Gold			1/4 yd.

Worsted-weight	Nylon Plus™	Need-loft™	YARN AMOUNT
Maple	#35	#13	18 yds.
White	#01	#41	10 yds.
Red	#19	#02	5 yds.
Royal	#09	#32	4 yds.
Gold	#27	#17	2 yds.
Black	#02	#00	1/4 yd.

STITCH KEY:
— Backstitch/Straight Stitch

A – Liberty Wreath Eagle
(cut 1)
33 x 90 holes

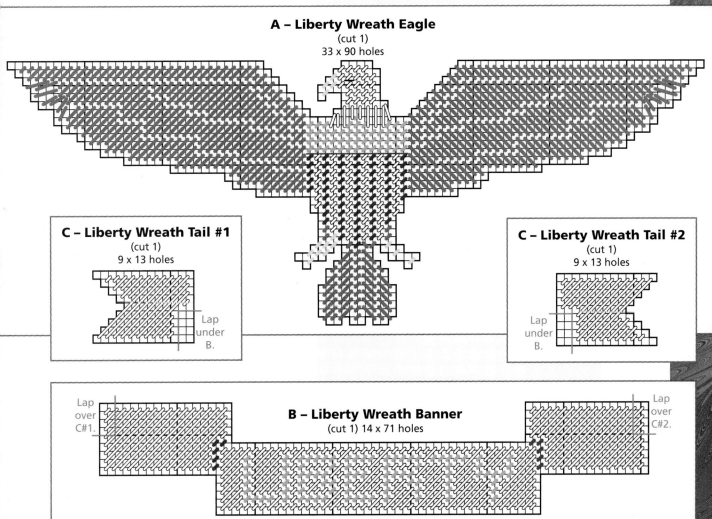

C – Liberty Wreath Tail #1
(cut 1)
9 x 13 holes

Lap under B.

C – Liberty Wreath Tail #2
(cut 1)
9 x 13 holes

Lap under B.

Lap over C#1.

B – Liberty Wreath Banner
(cut 1) 14 x 71 holes

Lap over C#2.

CELEBRATION GIFTS

Juicy watermelons are perfect for summer meals out-of-doors. Stitch this country-style set with strips of fabric and easy-to-stitch 5-count plastic canvas.

By Lilo Fruehwirth

Watermelon Picnic

CELEBRATION GIFTS

SIZE: Place Mat is 12" x 17¼"; Napkin Ring is 2" across; Basket is 6½" x 8" x 7½" tall, not including handle.

MATERIALS: Three sheets of 5-count plastic canvas; Sewing needle and matching color quilting thread; 44"-wide light-weight cotton fabric (for amounts see Color Key).

CUTTING INSTRUCTIONS: Graphs on pages 83-84.
 A: For Place Mat, cut one according to graph.
 B: For Napkin Ring, cut one 6 x 24 holes (no graph).
 C: For Basket sides and side linings, cut two each according to graphs.
 D: For Basket ends, cut two 21 x 31 holes.
 E: For Basket bottom, cut one 31 x 38 holes.
 F: For Basket handle, cut one 6 x 110 holes (no graph).

FABRIC PREPARATION INSTRUCTIONS:

1: If desired, prewash in cool water.

2: For fabric strips, measuring along one selvage edge of fabric, mark every ¾" and snip with sharp scissors to begin tear. (If selvage will not tear easily, trim off with scissors before snipping.)

3: Holding fabric firmly with both hands, starting at cut, tear into strips. Discard first and last strips if not correct width. Remove any long threads from strips.

STITCHING INSTRUCTIONS:

NOTES: To thread needle, fold one short end of strip in half and slide through eye of needle. Handle strips carefully to prevent excessive fraying.

1: Using colors and stitches indicated, work A, C, D and E pieces according to graphs. Using dk. green for Basket handle, lt. green print for Napkin ring and Long Stitch over narrow width, work B and F pieces, omitting first and last hole at each end of each piece. With dk. green, Overcast unfinished edges of A-E pieces; holding F pieces wrong sides together, Whipstitch together.

2: Holding short ends of B wrong sides together, sew together, forming cylinder.

3: For each Basket side, holding one side and one lining C wrong sides together, sew together.

4: Sew sides, D and E pieces together, forming Basket. With ends touching bottom, sew handle ends to inside of Basket as shown in photo. ▭

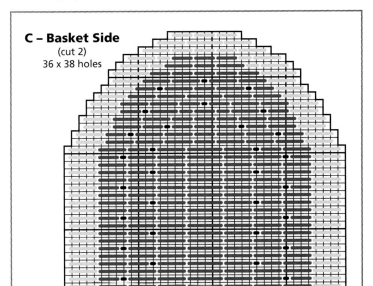

C – Basket Side
(cut 2)
36 x 38 holes

COLOR KEY: Watermelon Picnic

44"-wide cotton fabric	AMOUNT
Dk. Green	2 yds.
Red	1¼ yds.
Lt. Green print	½ yd.
Black	½ yd.

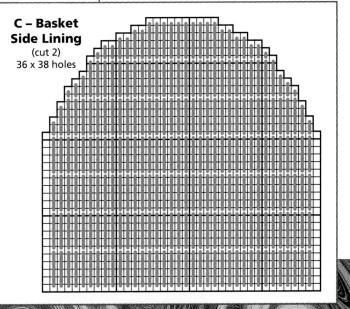

C – Basket Side Lining
(cut 2)
36 x 38 holes

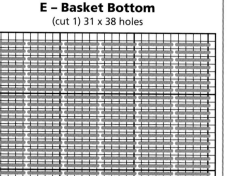

E – Basket Bottom
(cut 1) 31 x 38 holes

COLOR KEY: Watermelon Picnic

44"-wide cotton fabric	AMOUNT
Dk. Green	2 yds.
Red	1¼ yds.
Lt. Green print	½ yd.
Black	½ yd.

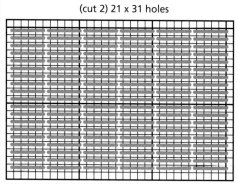

D – Basket End
(cut 2) 21 x 31 holes

A – Place Mat
(cut 1) 59 x 85 holes

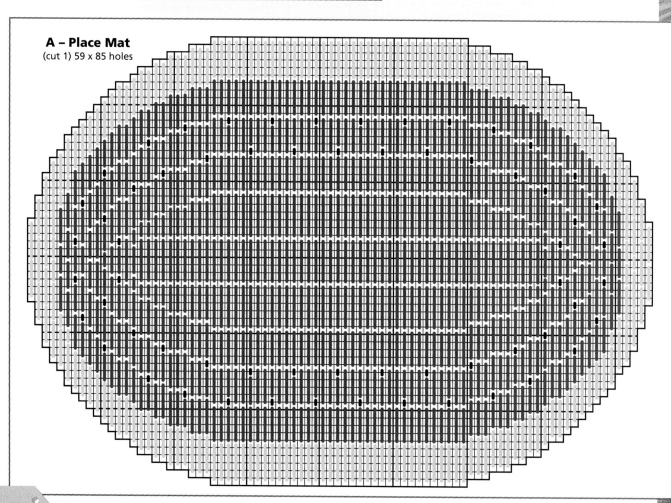

CELEBRATION GIFTS

SIZE: 11⅜" x 12¼".

MATERIALS: Three sheets of 7-count plastic canvas; One yellow/black 9-mm. animal eye; Brown fabric paint pen; Rose powdered cosmetic blush; Firm-hold hair spray; fire brown 8-mm. speckled artificial eggs; 2¼" bird nest; 1½" sawtooth hanger; ½" cardboard; Craft glue or glue gun; 6 yds. lime green six-strand embroidery floss; Worsted-weight or plastic canvas yarn (for amounts see Color Key on page 86).

CUTTING INSTRUCTIONS: Graphs on page 86.
    A: For wreath, cut two according to graph.
    B: For cardinal, cut one according to graph.
    C: For wing, cut one according to graph.
    D: For flowers, cut eleven according to graph.
    E: For leaves, cut fourteen according to graph.

STITCHING INSTRUCTIONS:

NOTES: To shape flowers and leaves before stitching, soak cut pieces in hot water; dip in cold water to set. For curved petals and leaves, pull any long stitches a bit tighter to help hold the shape. One A piece is unworked for backing.

1: Using colors and stitches indicated (use a doubled strand of red for diagonal stitches on wing), work one A and B-E pieces according to graphs. Fill in uncoded areas of B using red and Continental Stitch. Holding backing A to wrong side of worked piece, with camel, Whipstitch together. With matching colors, Overcast unfinished edges of B-E pieces.

2: With one finger, dust center of each flower petal with blush. Paint ends of each petal as shown in photo.

NOTE: Cut eleven 18" lengths of floss.

3: For each flower center, wrap one 18" length of floss around ½" cardboard 12-15 times. Tie loops together at one edge; cut through loops at opposite edge. Fluff and trim ends; spray with hair spray to stiffen.

4: Glue one flower center to each flower as shown. Cut shank off eye and glue to cardinal as indicated on graph; glue wing to cardinal as shown. Glue eggs inside nest and nest, cardinal, leaves and flowers to wreath as shown. Glue sawtooth hanger to wrong side.⌐

By Patricia Hall

Cardinal Wreath

This little fellow is "Home Tweet Home" amid dogwood blossoms on this cheerful wreath. It's an enchanting decoration for any season.

COLOR KEY: Cardinal Wreath

Worsted-weight	Nylon Plus™	Need-loft™	YARN AMOUNT
White	#01	#41	44 yds.
Camel	#34	#43	40 yds.
Mint	#30	#24	14 yds.
Red	#19	#02	10 yds.
Black	#02	#00	1 yd.
Dk. Orange	#18	#52	1 yd.

STITCH KEY:

○ Eye Attachment

E – Leaf
(cut 14)
5 x 11 holes

D – Flower
(cut 11)
15 x 15 holes

Cut Lines

C – Wing
(cut 1)
8 x 20 holes

A – Wreath
(cut 2) 64 x 64 holes

Cut Out

B – Cardinal
(cut 1)
21 x 42 holes

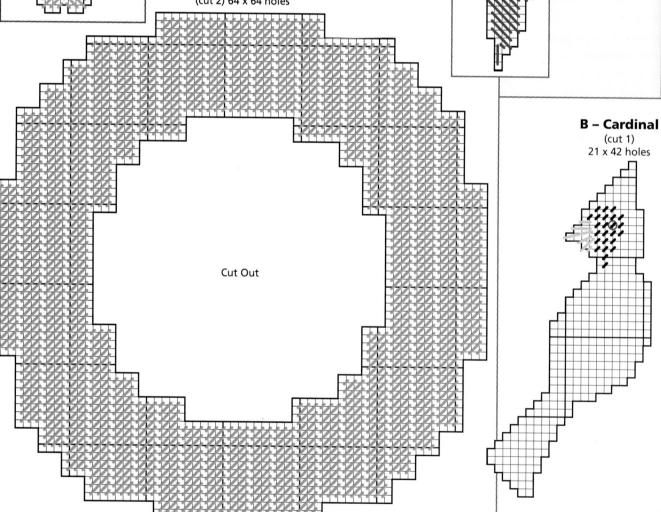

CELEBRATION GIFTS

Keep your needlework supplies together in this handy tote. It's the berries!

By Michele Wilcox

Berries & Birds Tote

Pattern begins next page

SIZE: 3⅛" x 13¾" x 10⅝" tall, not including handles.

MATERIALS: Three sheets of 7-count plastic canvas; Worsted-weight or plastic canvas yarn (for amounts see Color Key).

CUTTING INSTRUCTIONS:
A: For sides, use one 70 x 90-hole sheet for each.
B: For ends, cut two 20 x 70 holes.
C: For bottom, cut one 20 x 90 holes (no graph).
D: For handles, cut two 10 x 90 holes (no graph).

STITCHING INSTRUCTIONS:

NOTE: C piece is unworked.

1: Using colors indicated and Continental Stitch, work A, B and D pieces according to graphs and according to Handle Stitch Pattern Guide. Fill in uncoded areas using white and Continental Stitch. Using colors indicated and French Knot, embroider eyes as indicated on graph.

2: With white, Whipstitch A-C pieces together, forming tote. Overcast long edges of handles. Overcast unfinished edges of tote, catching short ends of each handle at opposite sides to join as indicated. ⬭

COLOR KEY: Berries & Birds Tote

	Worsted-weight	Nylon Plus™	Need-loft™	YARN AMOUNT
◼	White	#01	#41	5 oz.
◼	Dk. Red	#20	#01	2½ oz.
▨	Dk. Royal	#07	#48	2 oz.
▦	Green	#58	#28	2 oz.

STITCH KEY:
● French Knot

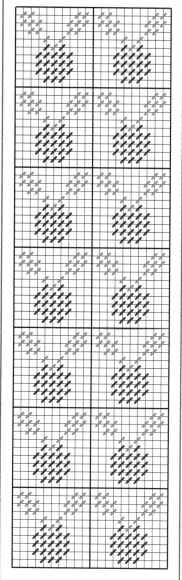

B – End
(cut 2) 20 x 70 holes

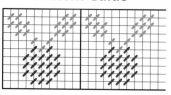

Handle Stitch Pattern Guide

Continue established pattern across each entire piece.

A – Side (70 x 90 holes)

Handle Attachment

Handle Attachment

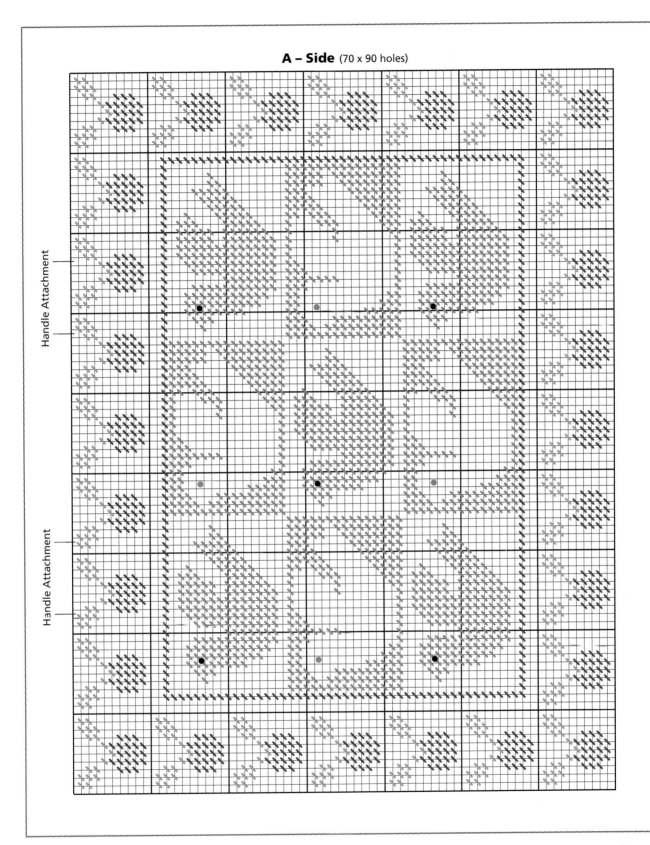

C E L E B R A T I O N   G I F T S

By Sandra Miller-Maxfield

Baby Gifts

Tiny teddy, pacifier and doorknob hanger make much-loved baby shower gifts. Stitch an extra pacifier, bottle, teddy or pin to use as package trim or magnet.

CELEBRATION GIFTS

BEAR RATTLE

SIZE: 3" x 5¼".

MATERIALS: ¼ sheet of 7-count plastic canvas; Two 3" plastic canvas radial circles; Four ½" animal eyes with shanks; Small jingle bell; Worsted-weight or plastic canvas yarn (for amounts see Color Key).

CUTTING INSTRUCTIONS:
A: For rattle, cut one according to graph.
B: For bear face, front and back, cut two according to graph.

STITCHING INSTRUCTIONS:

1: Using dusty blue and Continental Stitch, work A according to graph; Overcast unfinished edges.

2: Overlapping edges of one B piece as indicated on graph to form cone, using colors and stitches indicated, work muzzle from center according to graph, working through both thicknesses at overlap area to join.

3: Using cinnamon and Straight Stitch, embroider nose and mouth as shown in photo. Secure eyes with washers as shown. Repeat Steps 2 and 3 for remaining B piece.

4: Place one B piece on each side of A below ears, inserting bell. With lt. pink, Whipstitch A and B pieces together.

DOOR TAG & PACIFIER PIN

SIZE: Door Tag is 5" x 10¾"; Pacifier Pin is 1½" x 2⅜".

MATERIALS: One sheet of 7-count plastic canvas; 10" white ¼" satin ribbon; 1½" safety pin or pinback; Pacifier; Craft glue or glue gun; Worsted-weight or plastic canvas yarn (for amounts see Color Key on page 94).

CUTTING INSTRUCTIONS: Graphs on page 94.
A: For Door Tag, cut one according to graph.
B: For bottle, cut one according to graph.
C: For diaper pin, cut one according to graph.
D: For pacifier and Pacifier Pin, cut one each according to graph.

STITCHING INSTRUCTIONS:

1: Using colors indicated and Continental Stitch, work A-D pieces according to graphs. Fill in uncoded areas using lt. pink and Continental Stitch. Using black and Backstitch, embroider letters as indicated on graph.

2: With colors shown in photo, Overcast unfinished edges.

3: Glue bottle, diaper pin and pacifier to Door Tag as shown in photo.

4: For Pacifier Pin, glue pinback or stationary edge of safety pin to back. Glue ends of ribbon to back of Pacifier Pin. Using Lark's Head Knot, loop ribbon around handle of pacifier.

COLOR KEY: Bear Rattle

	Worsted-weight	Nylon Plus™	Need-loft™	YARN AMOUNT
■	Dusty Blue	#38	#34	10 yds.
■	Lt. Pink	#10	#08	10 yds.
□	Cinnamon	#44	#14	1½ yds.

A – Bear Rattle
(cut 1) 16 x 33 holes

Cut Out

Cut Out

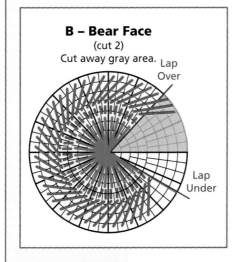

B – Bear Face
(cut 2)
Cut away gray area.
Lap Over

Lap Under

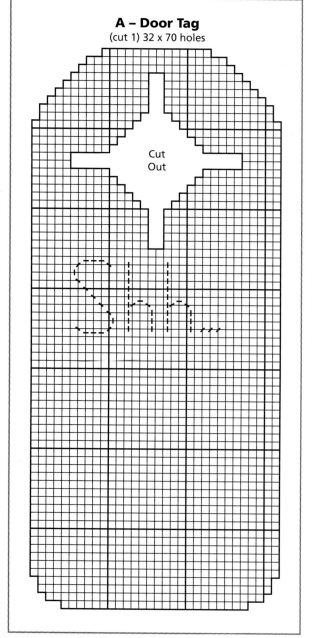

A – Door Tag
(cut 1) 32 x 70 holes

Cut Out

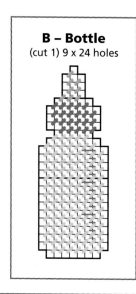

B – Bottle
(cut 1) 9 x 24 holes

D – Pacifier & Pacifier Pin
(cut 1 each) 9 x 15 holes

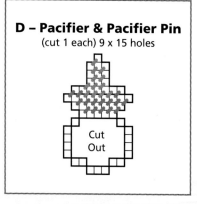

Cut Out

COLOR KEY: Door Tag & Pin

	Worsted-weight	Nylon Plus™	Need-loft™	YARN AMOUNT
	Lt. Pink	#10	#08	42 yds.
	Lt. Blue	#05	#36	5 yds.
	Sail Blue	#04	#35	4 yds.
	Peach	#46	#47	2 yds.
	Silver	#40	#37	2 yds.
	Black	#02	#00	1 yd.
	Flesh	#14	#56	1 yd.

STITCH KEY:

— Backstitch/Straight Stitch

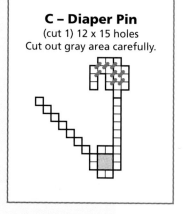

C – Diaper Pin
(cut 1) 12 x 15 holes
Cut out gray area carefully.

Carry on the tradition of sampler stitching to record a family birth. Personalize this colorful sampler with the new baby's name, date of birth and weight.

BABY'S NAME
12·30·00
00 LBS. 00 OZ.

By Lois Winston

Baby's Here!

Pattern begins next page

SIZE: 8" x 10".

MATERIALS: One sheet of 10-count plastic canvas; Frame of choice; #3 pearl cotton or six-strand embroidery floss (for amounts see Color Key).

CUTTING INSTRUCTIONS:
   A: For sampler, cut one 79 x 99 holes.

STITCHING INSTRUCTIONS:

1: Using colors indicated and Continental Stitch, work A according to graph and according to Sampler Alphabet & Number Graph (work letters of choice for baby's name, birth date and weight, centered as indicated on graph). Fill in uncoded areas using white and Continental Stitch. Using pearl cotton or six strands floss in colors indicated and French Knot, embroider eyes and noses as indicated.

2: Do not Overcast unfinished edges.

3: Frame as desired.

COLOR KEY: Baby's Here!

#3 pearl cotton or floss		AMOUNT
☐	White	100 yds.
▨	Lt. Blue	8 yds.
▨	Dk. Blue	6 yds.
▨	Yellow	6 yds.
▨	Lt. Violet	4 yds.
■	Dk. Pink	3 yds.
▨	Lt. Pink	3 yds.
■	Black	2 yds.
▨	Dk. Green	2 yds.
▨	Dk. Violet	2 yds.
▨	Lt. Green	2 yds.
▨	Orange	1 yd.

STITCH KEY:
● French Knot

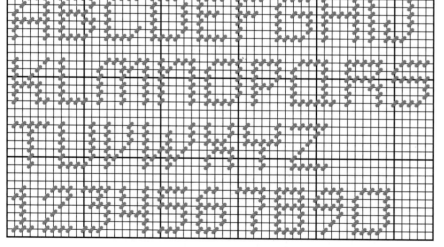

Sampler Alphabet & Letter Graph

ut 1) 79 x 99 holes

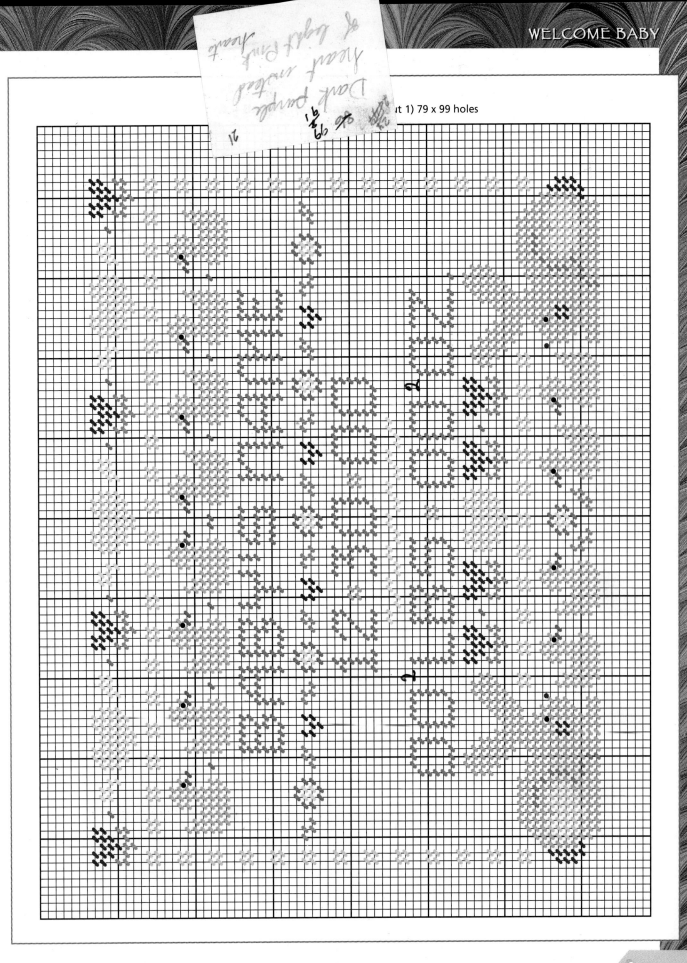

CELEBRATION GIFTS

Baby carriages will hold mints or nuts at a
shower, and later, they'll hold pins or cotton
balls in the nursery. Proudly display the
carriage photo frame in your home or office.

CELEBRATION GIFTS

By Jocelyn Sass

Carriage Ride

CARRIAGE

SIZE: 3¾" x 6" x 7" tall, not including handle.

MATERIALS FOR ONE: One sheet of 12" x 18" or larger 7-count plastic canvas; Eight 3" plastic canvas circles; Worsted-weight or plastic canvas yarn (for amounts see Color Keys on page 100).

CUTTING INSTRUCTIONS FOR ONE: Graphs and diagram on pages 100-101.
A: For sides, cut two according to Boy or Girl graph.
B: For bottom and hood, cut one 24 x 102 holes (no graph).
C: For wheels, use canvas circles.
D: For handle, cut one 3 x 44 holes (no graph).

STITCHING INSTRUCTIONS:

1: Using colors indicated and Continental Stitch, work one A piece according to Boy or Girl graph. Fill in uncoded areas and work remaining A (on opposite side of canvas) and B pieces using white and Continental Stitch. Using colors indicated for Boy Carriage or substituting pink for lt. blue and lilac for sail blue for Girl Carriage and Long Stitch, work C pieces according to graph. For each wheel, holding two C pieces wrong sides together, with matching colors, Whipstitch together.

2: Using lt. blue for Boy or pink for Girl and Slanted Gobelin Stitch over narrow width, work D. With sail blue for Boy or lilac for Girl, Overcast unfinished edges of handle.

3: Holding A pieces wrong sides together with B between, with white, Whipstitch together according to Carriage Assembly Diagram. With white, Overcast unfinished edges of Carriage. Using sail blue for Boy or lilac for Girl and Cross Stitch for wheels and Straight Stitch for handle, attach each wheel center and short ends of handle to Carriage as indicated.

FRAME

SIZE: 6⅝" x 6⅞" tall, not including handle.

MATERIALS: One sheet of 7-count plastic canvas; Two 3" plastic canvas circles; One sawtooth hanger; Craft glue or glue gun; Worsted-weight or plastic canvas yarn (for amounts see Color Keys on page 101).

CUTTING INSTRUCTIONS:
A: For frame front and back, cut one each according to graph on page 101.
B: For handle, cut one 3 x 31 holes (no graph).
C: For wheels, use canvas circles.

STITCHING INSTRUCTIONS:

1: Using colors indicated for Girl Frame, or substituting lt. blue for pink and sail blue for lilac for Boy Frame and Continental Stitch, work front A according to graph. Fill in uncoded areas using white and Continental Stitch. Using lilac and Continental Stitch, work back A on opposite side of canvas. Using pink for Girl or lt. blue for Boy and Slanted Gobelin Stitch over narrow width, work B. Using colors indicated for Boy, or substituting pink for lt. blue and lilac for sail blue for Girl, and Long Stitch, work C pieces according to graph.

2: With white, Overcast unfinished cutout edges of front A. With lilac for Girl or sail blue for Boy, Overcast unfinished edges of B and C pieces.

3: Holding A pieces wrong sides together, with lilac for Girl or sail blue for Boy, Whipstitch together, leaving top edge unjoined as indicated on graph; Overcast unfinished edges. Using above colors and Cross Stitch for wheels and Straight Stitch for handles, attach center of each wheel and short ends of handle to frame as indicated. Glue hanger to top center back of Frame. ▱

COLOR KEY: Girl Carriage

Worsted-weight	Nylon Plus™	Need-loft™	YARN AMOUNT
White	#01	#41	2 oz.
Lilac	#22	#45	28 yds.
Pink	#11	#07	28 yds.

STITCH KEY:
◆ Handle Attachment
✕ Wheel Attachment

COLOR KEY: Boy Carriage

Worsted-weight	Nylon Plus™	Need-loft™	YARN AMOUNT
White	#01	#41	2 oz.
Lt. Blue	#05	#36	28 yds.
Sail Blue	#04	#35	28 yds.

STITCH KEY:
◆ Handle Attachment
✕ Wheel Attachment

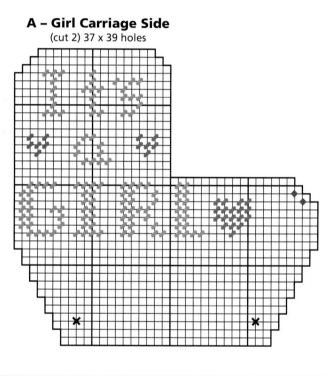

A – Girl Carriage Side
(cut 2) 37 x 39 holes

A – Boy Carriage Side
(cut 2) 37 x 39 holes

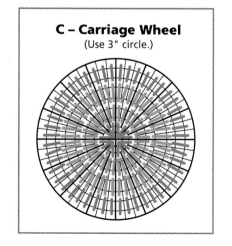

C – Carriage Wheel
(Use 3" circle.)

COLOR KEY: Girl Frame

	Worsted-weight	Nylon Plus™	Need-loft™	YARN AMOUNT
	Lilac	#22	#45	34 yds.
	White	#01	#41	18 yds.
	Pink	#11	#07	9 yds.

STITCH KEY:
◆ Handle Attachment
✕ Wheel Attachment

Carriage Assembly Diagram

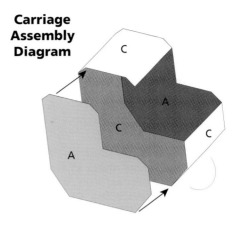

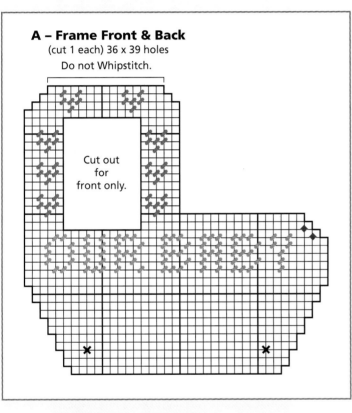

A – Frame Front & Back
(cut 1 each) 36 x 39 holes
Do not Whipstitch.

Cut out for front only.

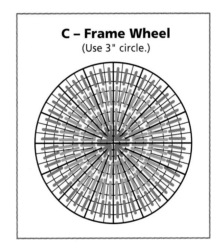

C – Frame Wheel
(Use 3" circle.)

COLOR KEY: Boy Frame

	Worsted-weight	Nylon Plus™	Need-loft™	YARN AMOUNT
	Sail Blue	#04	#35	34 yds.
	White	#01	#41	18 yds.
	Lt. Blue	#05	#36	9 yds.

STITCH KEY:
◆ Handle Attachment
✕ Wheel Attachment

CELEBRATION GIFTS

By Sandra Miller-Maxfield

Jolly Jack

SIZE: 4" x 4" x 9½" tall.

MATERIALS: Two sheets of 7-count plastic canvas; One sheet of flexible 7-count plastic canvas; Two red ¾" pom-poms; Eight clothespins; Craft glue or glue gun; Polyester fiberfill, marbles or gravel (optional); Worsted-weight or plastic canvas yarn (for amounts see Color Key on page 105).

CUTTING INSTRUCTIONS FOR BOX: Graphs and diagram on pages 104-105.
A: For front, cut one 24 x 24 holes.
B: For back, cut one 24 x 24 holes.
C: For left side, cut one 24 x 24 holes.
D: For right side, cut one 24 x 24 holes.
E: For lid, cut one 24 x 24 holes.
F: For lid liner, cut one 24 x 24 holes (no graph).
G: For bottom, cut one 24 x 24 holes (no graph).

CUTTING INSTRUCTIONS FOR JACK:
NOTE: Use flexible canvas for E pieces.
A: For face, cut one according to graph.
B: For head edge, cut one 5 x 70 holes.
C: For back of head, cut one according to graph.
D: For hands, cut two according to graph.
E: For body piece, cut four according to graph.

STITCHING INSTRUCTIONS FOR BOX:

1: Using colors indicated and Continental Stitch, work A-E pieces according to graphs. Using red and French Knot, embroider hair on A piece as indicated on graph. Fill in uncoded areas using lt. blue and Continental Stitch.

2: Using lt. blue and Continental Stitch, work F. Using lt. blue and Slanted Gobelin Stitch over four bars, work G piece.

3: With lt. blue, Whipstitch A-D and G pieces together, forming box. Holding E and F wrong sides together, Whipstitch three sides together as indicated on E graph.

Whipstitch unfinished edges of lid to back of box, leaving box open; Overcast unfinished edges.

4: Glue pom-pom to clown face as indicated.

STITCHING INSTRUCTIONS FOR JACK:

1: Carefully fan fold E pieces at each shallow and deep notch according to Body Folding Diagram; secure with clothespins to mold shape. Set aside.

2: Using colors indicated and Continental Stitch, work A-D (one D on oppostite side of canvas) pieces according to graphs. Using gold and French Knot, embroider hair on B and C pieces as indicated.

3: To shape cheeks on A and C pieces, with white, Whipstitch X edges together as indicated.

4: With matching colors, Overcast unfinished edges of D pieces.

5: Unpin E pieces. Using colors indicated and Slanted Gobelin Stitch, work E pieces according to graph. Being careful to keep folds intact, with matching colors, Whipstitch side edges together, forming body. Secure folds on inside with glue as needed.

6: Glue pom-pom to face as indicated. Glue hands to body and head to center top of body as shown in photo. If desired, fill box with fiberfill, gravel, or marbles. Carefully glue body inside box as shown. ⬚

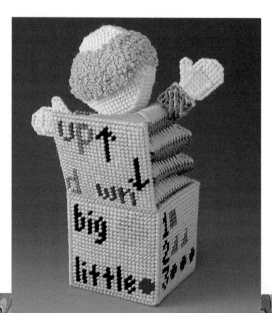

CELEBRATION GIFTS

Children love this cheery, fun-to-make jack-in-the-box. He's educational, too — teach your little one "up," "down," "big," and "little," as well as his first numbers.

E – Body Piece
(cut 4 from flexible canvas)
34 x 34 holes

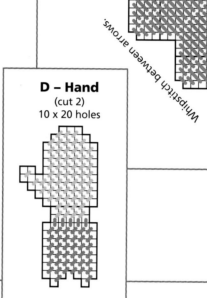

Neck Edge

Neck Edge

Whipstitch between arrows.

Whipstitch between arrows.

Body Folding
Diagram

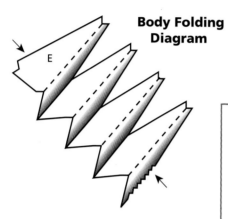

E

D – Hand
(cut 2)
10 x 20 holes

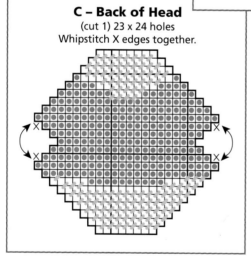

C – Back of Head
(cut 1) 23 x 24 holes
Whipstitch X edges together.

A – Face
(cut 1) 23 x 24 holes
Whipstitch X edges together.

B – Head Edge (cut 1) 5 x 70 holes

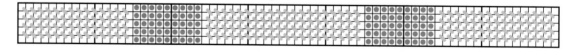

A – Box Front
(cut 1) 24 x 24 holes

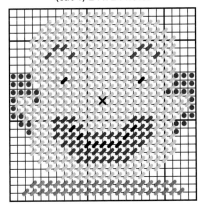

B – Box Back
(cut 1) 24 x 24 holes

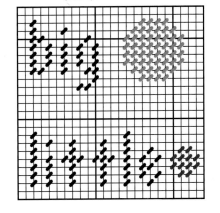

C – Box Left Side
(cut 1) 24 x 24 holes

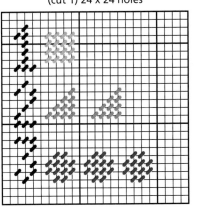

D – Box Right Side
(cut 1) 24 x 24 holes

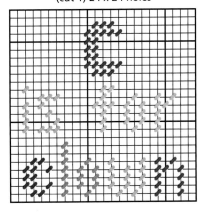

E – Box Lid
(cut 1) 24 x 24 holes

Whipstitch to F.

Whipstitch to F.

Whipstitch to F.

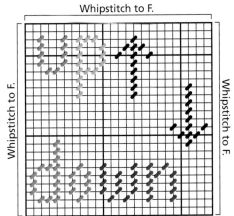

COLOR KEY: Jolly Jack

	Worsted-weight	Nylon Plus™	Need-loft™	YARN AMOUNT
	Lt. Blue	#05	#36	2 oz.
	Green	#58	#28	21 yds.
	Tangerine	#15	#11	21 yds.
	White	#01	#41	21 yds.
	Black	#02	#00	10 yds.
	Purple	#21	#46	10 yds.
	Red	#19	#02	10 yds.
	Turquoise	#03	#54	10 yds.
	Rust	#51	#09	2 yds.

STITCH KEY:

●   French Knot

✕   Pom-pom Placement

FALL
HARVEST

CELEBRATION GIFTS

Herald the arrival of
autumn with a medley of
harvest treasures. Gobbler
tissue cover, autumn
magnets and decorated
harvest brooms make
great hostess gifts.

Autumn Accents

CELEBRATION GIFTS

GOBBLER TISSUE COVER
By Michele Wilcox

SIZE: Loosely covers a boutique-style tissue box.

MATERIALS: Two sheets of 7-count plastic canvas; Velcro® closure (optional); Craft glue or glue gun; Six-strand embroidery floss (for amount see Color Key); Worsted-weight or plastic canvas yarn (for amounts see Color Key).

CUTTING INSTRUCTIONS: Diagrams and graphs continued on page 110.
A: **For sides, cut four 30 x 36 holes.**
B: **For top, cut one according to graph.**
C: **For optional cover bottom and flap, cut one 30 x 30 holes and one 12 x 30 holes (no graphs).**

D: **For tail, cut one according to graph.**
E: **For body, cut one according to graph.**
F: **For wings, cut two according to graph.**

STITCHING INSTRUCTIONS:

1: Using colors and stitches indicated, work A, B and D-F pieces according to graphs. Fill in uncoded areas of E using beige and Continental Stitch. Using dk. red and Continental Stitch, work F pieces on opposite sides of canvas.

2: Using cinnamon for tail, pumpkin for feet and with matching colors, Overcast unfinished edges of D-F pieces. Using six strands floss, Straight Stitch and French Knot, embroider eyes as indicated on graph.

3: With pumpkin, Overcast unfinished cutout edges of top. Whipstitch A and B pieces together, forming cover.

4: For optional cover bottom, Whipstitch unworked C pieces together at one matching edge according to Optional Cover Bottom Assembly Diagram. Whipstitch opposite edge of bottom to one side of cover; Overcast unfinished edges. Glue tail, wings and body to cover as shown in photo. If desired, glue closure to flap and inside of cover.

COLOR KEY: Gobbler Tissue Cover

Embroidery floss			AMOUNT
■ Black			½ yd.

Worsted-weight	Nylon Plus™	Need-loft™	YARN AMOUNT
Rust	#51	#09	60 yds.
Beige	#43	#40	54 yds.
Pumpkin	#50	#12	42 yds.
Cinnamon	#44	#14	10 yds.
Dk. Red	#20	#01	4 yds.

STITCH KEY:
— Backstitch/Straight Stitch
● French Knot

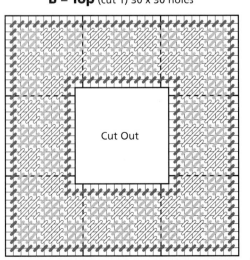

B – Top (cut 1) 30 x 30 holes

Cut Out

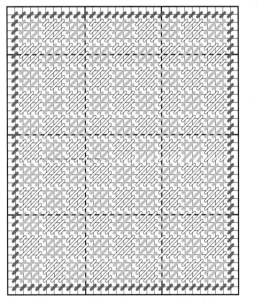

A – Side (cut 4) 30 x 36 holes

Optional Cover Bottom Assembly Diagram

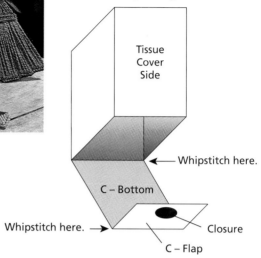

Tissue Cover Side

Whipstitch here.

C – Bottom

Whipstitch here. →

Closure

C – Flap

D – Tail
(cut 1) 32 x 36 holes

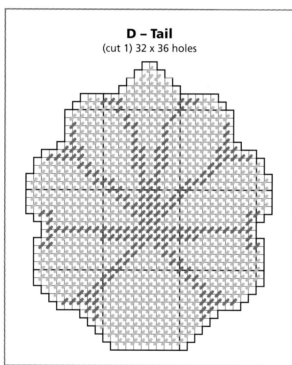

COLOR KEY: Gobbler Tissue Cover

Embroidery floss			AMOUNT
Black			1/2 yd.

Worsted-weight	Nylon Plus™	Need-loft™	YARN AMOUNT
Rust	#51	#09	60 yds.
Beige	#43	#40	54 yds.
Pumpkin	#50	#12	42 yds.
Cinnamon	#44	#14	10 yds.
Dk. Red	#20	#01	4 yds.

STITCH KEY:
— Backstitch/Straight Stitch
● French Knot

F – Wing
(cut 2)
9 x 13 holes

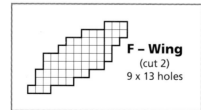

E – Body
(cut 1)
14 x 29 holes

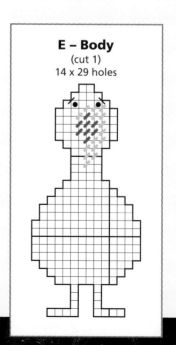

DECORATIVE BROOMS
By Catherine Bihlmaier

SIZE: Large Broom is 6⅝" x 22½"; Small Broom is 4⅝" x 18¼".

MATERIALS: One sheet of 13½" x 22½" 7-count plastic canvas; One sheet of 12" x 18" or larger 7-count plastic canvas; 4½ yds. red ⅜" ribbon; Dried flower spray and pinecones (optional); Craft glue or glue gun; Worsted-weight or plastic canvas yarn (for amounts see Color Key).

CUTTING INSTRUCTIONS:
A: For Large Broom, cut two according to graph.
B: For Small Broom, cut two according to graph.

STITCHING INSTRUCTIONS:

NOTES: Use a doubled strand of yarn for straw and binding and a single strand for handles. One A and one B piece are unworked for backings.

1: Using colors and stitches indicated, work one A (straw first, then binding and handle) and one B piece according to graphs, continuing Slanted Gobelin Stitch for entire length of each handle as indicated on graphs.

2: Holding backing A and B pieces to wrong sides of matching worked pieces, with matching colors, Whipstitch together.

NOTE: Cut one 1½-yd. length and one 3-yd. length of ribbon.

4: Tie short length of ribbon into a decorative bow around base of Small Broom as shown in photo. Beginning at top, wrap remaining ribbon around handle of Large Broom; tie into a decorative bow as shown. If desired, glue pinecones and dried flower spray to bow.

COLOR KEY: Brooms

	Worsted-weight	Nylon Plus™	Need-loft™	YARN AMOUNT
	Gold	#27	#17	2 oz.
	Cinnamon	#44	#14	63 yds.

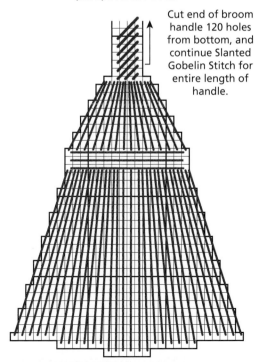

B – Small Broom
(cut 2) 30 x 120 holes

Cut end of broom handle 120 holes from bottom, and continue Slanted Gobelin Stitch for entire length of handle.

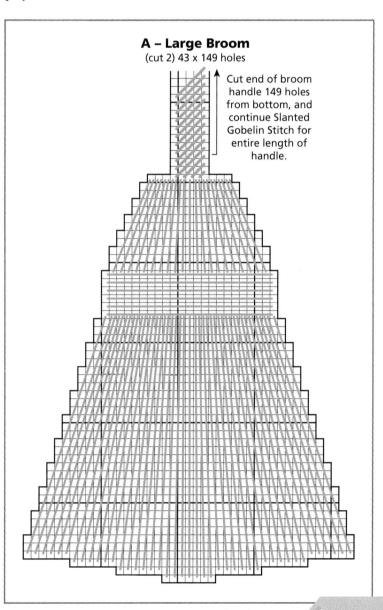

A – Large Broom
(cut 2) 43 x 149 holes

Cut end of broom handle 149 holes from bottom, and continue Slanted Gobelin Stitch for entire length of handle.

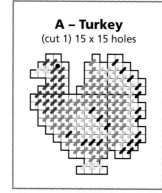

A – Turkey
(cut 1) 15 x 15 holes

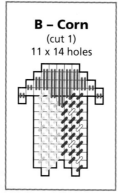

B – Corn
(cut 1)
11 x 14 holes

COLOR KEY: Harvest Magnets

	Worsted-weight	Nylon Plus™	Need-loft™	YARN AMOUNT
	Maple	#35	#13	3 yds.
	Burgundy	#13	#03	2½ yds.
	Tangerine	#15	#11	2 yds.
	Dk. Orange	#18	#52	1½ yds.
	Sand	#47	#16	1½ yds.
	Black	#02	#00	1 yd.
	White	#01	#41	¼ yd.

STITCH KEY:
● French Knot

HARVEST MAGNETS
By Margaret Saack

SIZE: Turkey is 2⅜" x 2⅜"; Corn is 1¾" x 2⅜".

MATERIALS: Scraps of 7-count plastic canvas; ⅓ yd. orange ¹⁄₁₆" satin ribbon; Magnetic strips; Craft glue or glue gun; Worsted-weight or plastic canvas yarn (for amounts see Color Key).

CUTTING INSTRUCTIONS:
A: For Turkey, cut one according to graph.
B: For Corn, cut one according to graph.

STITCHING INSTRUCTIONS:

NOTE: Untwist sand yarn before stitching husks on B.

1: Using colors and stitches indicated, work A and B pieces according to graphs. With maple for feathers and with matching colors, Overcast unfinished edges. Using black and French Knot, embroider eye as indicated on A graph.

NOTE: Cut one 3" length of ribbon.

2: Glue ends of 3" ribbon to back of Corn as shown in photo. Tie remaining ribbon into a bow; trim ends. Glue bow to front as shown. ▱

CELEBRATION GIFTS

By Carolyn Christmas

Mallards & Cattails

Dad will love desk accessories
created especially for him.
Tissue cover keeps
tissues handy in style, and
bookend cover slips over a
standard metal bookend.

Pattern begins next page

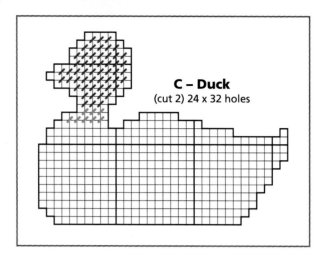

C – Duck
(cut 2) 24 x 32 holes

SIZE: Tissue Cover snugly covers a boutique-style tissue box; Bookend Cover is 5¾" x 5¾" and slips over a standard-size metal bookend.

MATERIALS: Three sheets of 7-count plastic canvas; One metal bookend; Craft glue or glue gun; Worsted-weight or plastic canvas yarn (for amounts see Color Key).

CUTTING INSTRUCTIONS:
A: For tissue cover top, cut one according to graph.
B: For tissue cover sides, cut four 30 x 37 holes.
C: For ducks, cut two according to graph.
D: For cattails, cut four according to graph.
E: For bookend cover front and back, cut one each according to graphs.

STITCHING INSTRUCTIONS:

1: Using colors and stitches indicated, work A-D and front E piece according to graphs. Fill in uncoded areas of ducks using dk. royal and cattails using maple and Continental Stitch. With matching colors, Overcast unfinished cutout edges of A and outer edges of C and D pieces.

2: With eggshell, Whipstitch A and B pieces together, forming tissue cover; Overcast unfinished edges.

3: With eggshell, holding unworked back E to wrong side of front E and matching top edges, Whipstitch together, forming bookend cover as indicated; Overcast remaining unfinished edges of front.

4: Glue cattails and ducks to covers as shown in photo.

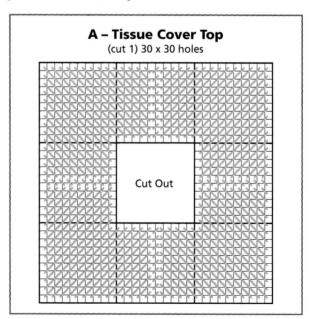

A – Tissue Cover Top
(cut 1) 30 x 30 holes

Cut Out

D – Cattail
(cut 4) 5 x 25 holes

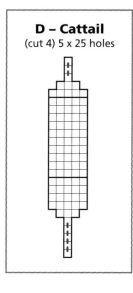

E – Bookend Cover Back
(cut 1) 24 x 37 holes

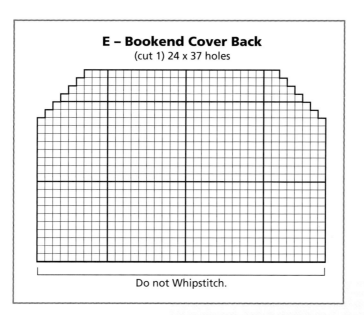

Do not Whipstitch.

E – Bookend Cover Front
(cut 1) 37 x 37 holes

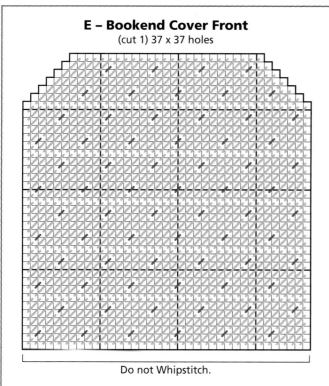

Do not Whipstitch.

COLOR KEY: Mallards & Cattails

	Worsted-weight	Nylon Plus™	Need-loft™	YARN AMOUNT
	Eggshell	#24	#39	3 oz.
	Dk. Royal	#07	#48	24 yds.
	Tan	#33	#18	11 yds.
	Maple	#35	#13	8 yds.
	Rust	#51	#09	4 yds.
	Cinnamon	#44	#14	2 yds.
	Green	#58	#28	1 yd.

B – Tissue Cover Side
(cut 4) 30 x 37 holes

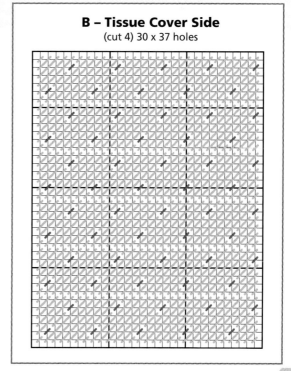

By Trudy Bath Smith

Bountiful Harvest

SIZE: Each standing figure is about 8½" tall on a 5¾" x 6" base; Canoe is 2⅝" x 12½" x 4¾" tall.

MATERIALS: Three sheets of 7-count plastic canvas; Two sheets of beige 7-count plastic canvas; Two small glass votive candle cups with candles (optional); Craft glue or glue gun; Worsted-weight or plastic canvas yarn (for amounts see Color Key on page 118).

CUTTING INSTRUCTIONS: Graphs on pages 118 – 119.
NOTE: Use beige canvas for girl, boy and base backings.
A: For girl, cut one from each color according to graph.
B: For boy, cut one from each color according to graph.
C: For bases, cut two from each color according to graph.
D: For girl's basket, cut one according to graph.
E: For boy's basket, cut one according to graph.
F: For canoe sides, cut two according to graph.
G: For canoe bottom, cut one according to graph.

STITCHING INSTRUCTIONS:

NOTE: Backing pieces are unworked.

1: Using colors and stitches indicated, work A-F pieces according to graphs, leaving uncoded areas of C pieces unworked. Fill in uncoded areas of F pieces and work G using maple and Continental Stitch.

2: Using colors indicated, French Knot, Backstitch,

Straight Stitch, Lazy Daisy Stitch and Lark's Head Knot, embroider detail as indicated on graphs. With maple for top and bottom and aqua for sides, Overcast unfinished edges of girl's basket. With crimson for top, maple for upper sides and with matching colors, Overcast unfinished edges of boy's basket.

NOTES: Cut two 8" lengths each of crimson, aqua and lt. yellow for headbands. Cut six 12" and two 6" lengths of black and two 4" lengths of crimson for braids and ties.

3: For each headband, braid one 8" length of each color together. Tie one headband around each head as shown in photo; knot on wrong side and trim ends of tie. For each braid, tie three 12" lengths together in center with one 6" length; knot and trim ends. Holding two lengths together for each strand, braid from knot to about 1" from ends. Wrap one 4" length around end as shown; knot and trim or glue ends to secure.

4: For each figure, holding backing to wrong side of matching worked piece, with lt. yellow for edges of clothing and with matching colors, Whipstitch together as indicated, catching knotted end of one braid at each ear area on girl as you work. With lt. yellow for girl and maple for boy, Whipstitch open bottom edges of each figure to corresponding base at unworked area. For each base, holding one backing C to wrong side of one worked piece, with forest, Whipstitch together. Glue baskets to figures as shown.

5: Holding F pieces wrong sides together, with maple, Whipstitch together as indicated. Whipstitch open bottom edges of canoe sides and G together; Overcast unfinished edges of canoe. If desired, place votive cup on base behind figure. ▱

CELEBRATION GIFTS

Celebrate the harvest with these whimsical Native American-inspired table decorations. Little boy and girl are candle holders, while canoe holds nuts or other treats.

COLOR KEY: Bountiful Harvest

Worsted-weight	Nylon Plus™	Need-loft™	YARN AMOUNT
Maple	#35	#13	2 oz.
Forest	#32	#29	36 yds.
Lt. Yellow	#42	#21	30 yds.
Crimson	#53	#42	12 yds.
Brown	#36	#15	10 yds.
Flesh	#14	#56	10 yds.
Black	#02	#00	8 yds.
Aqua	#60	#51	7 yds.

STITCH KEY:

— Backstitch/Straight Stitch
● French Knot
○ Lark's Head Knot
⬭ Lazy Daisy Stitch

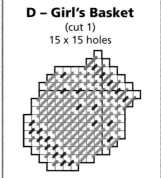

D – Girl's Basket
(cut 1)
15 x 15 holes

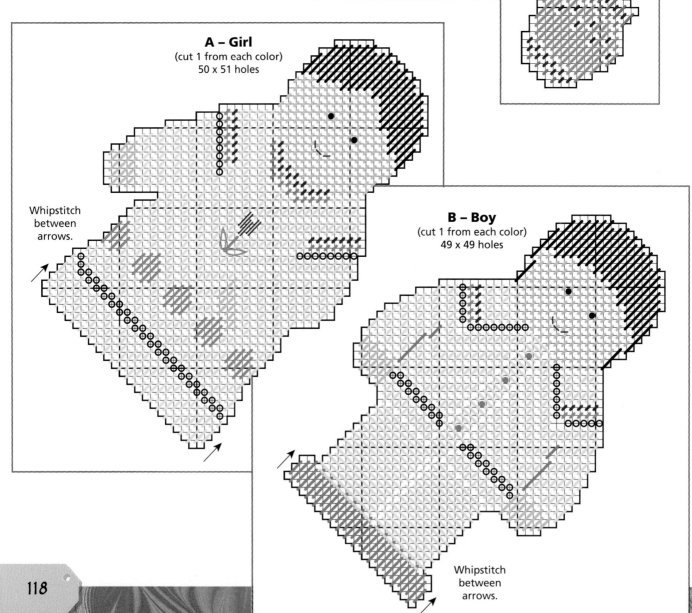

A – Girl
(cut 1 from each color)
50 x 51 holes

Whipstitch between arrows.

B – Boy
(cut 1 from each color)
49 x 49 holes

Whipstitch between arrows.

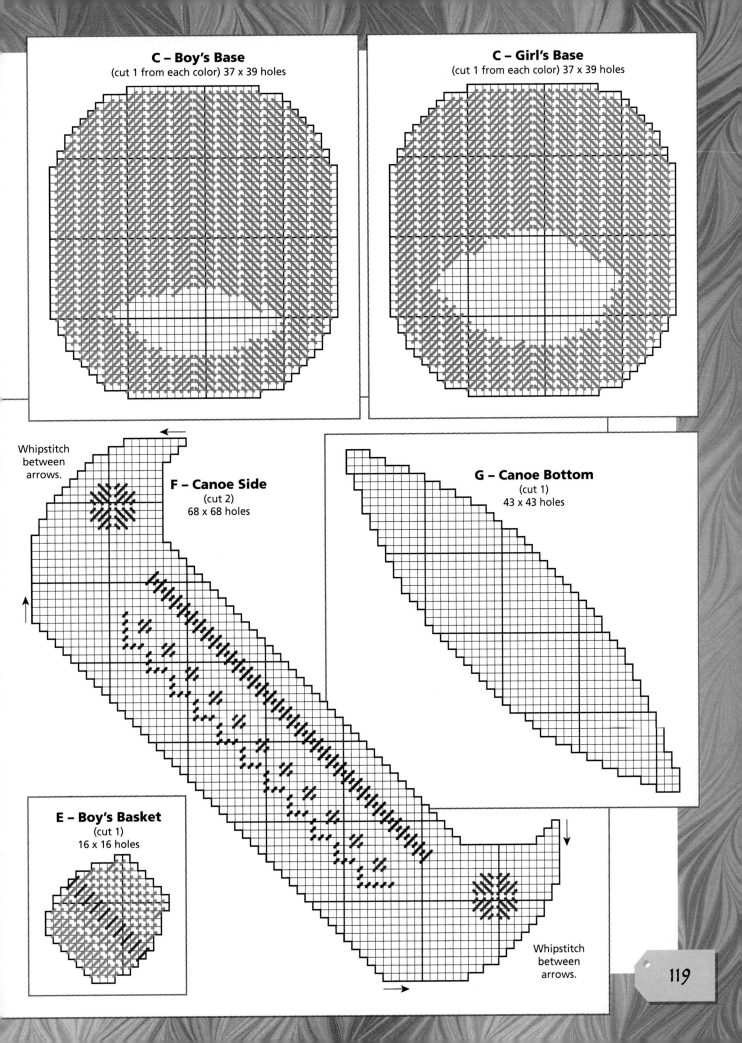

C – Boy's Base
(cut 1 from each color) 37 x 39 holes

C – Girl's Base
(cut 1 from each color) 37 x 39 holes

Whipstitch between arrows.

F – Canoe Side
(cut 2)
68 x 68 holes

G – Canoe Bottom
(cut 1)
43 x 43 holes

E – Boy's Basket
(cut 1)
16 x 16 holes

Whipstitch between arrows.

119

CELEBRATION GIFTS

Decorate your door with colorful corn you can use year after year! Twisted paper forms shucks and a perky bow. Corn is beautiful alone or on a grapevine wreath, as shown.

By Fran Rohus

Colorful Corn

CELEBRATION GIFTS

SIZE: Each ear of corn is about 6¼" long.

MATERIALS: Three sheets of 7-count plastic canvas; 12½"-across grapevine wreath; Several yds. each of rust and beige twisted paper; Stapler (optional); Craft glue or glue gun; Worsted-weight or plastic canvas yarn (for amounts see Color Key).

CUTTING INSTRUCTIONS:
A: For ears, cut three according to graph.
B: For ear tops, cut three according to graph.

STITCHING INSTRUCTIONS:

1: Using colors and stitches indicated, work A pieces according to graph, leaving indicated areas unworked. Holding bottom X edges wrong sides together, with gold and beginning as indicated on graph, Whipstitch together, lapping unworked tab under work at seam.

2: Whipstitch seam together as indicated, then Whipstitch top X edges together. Using gold and Continental Stitch, work B pieces. For each ear of corn, Whipstitch one A and one B together as indicated on B graph. Whipstitch bottom edges of ear together to cover.

NOTES: Cut nine 7" lengths of beige and one 18" length of rust twisted paper. Trim 7" lengths of beige to look like husks.

3: For each ear, staple or glue edges of short ends of three husks together. Glue stapled end to ear top; open paper folds. Tie 18" length of rust twisted paper into bow; trim ends. Wrap wreath with rust as shown in photo; glue ends to secure. Glue ears of corn to wreath and bow to corn as shown.

COLOR KEY: Colorful Corn

Worsted-weight	Nylon Plus™	Need-loft™	YARN AMOUNT
Gold	#27	#17	2½ oz.
Taupe	#16	#10	30 yds.
Cinnamon	#44	#14	30 yds.

STITCH KEY:
☐ Unworked Area
— Seam Line

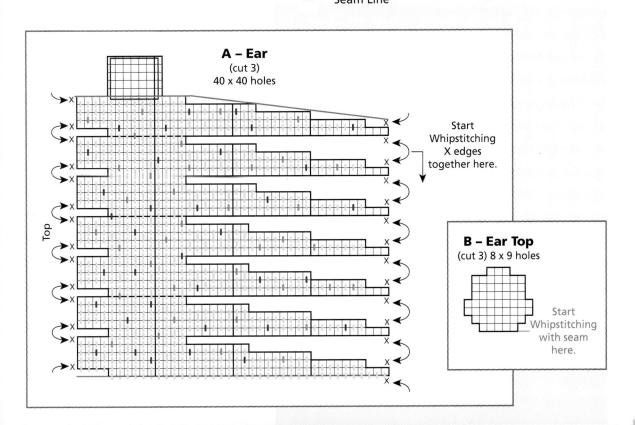

A – Ear
(cut 3)
40 x 40 holes

Start Whipstitching X edges together here.

Top

B – Ear Top
(cut 3) 8 x 9 holes

Start Whipstitching with seam here.

WINTER
FESTIVITIES

This sugarplum house is a tempting confection
of lace, beads and peppermint trims. Lift the
roof and – surprise! – it's a candy dish
for holding real treats.

CELEBRATION GIFTS

By Gina Woods

Gingerbread House

SIZE: 5½" x 9" x 8" tall.

MATERIALS: Three sheets of 7-count plastic canvas; ½ sheet of white 7-count plastic canvas; One 3" plastic canvas radial circle; Four green and two white 20-mm. star beads; Two each green, red and white 12-mm. star beads; One green 6-mm. faceted bead; 67 assorted-color 4-mm. faceted beads; 21 silver 3-mm. round beads; ½ yd. white ¼" sculpted lace with 3/8"-apart motifs; 9" white ½" pre-gathered lace; Scraps of white ⅝" edging lace; 6" white chenille stem; Polyester fiberfill; Sewing needle and white thread; Crystal glitter (optional); Craft glue or glue gun; 4-ply or worsted-weight yarn (for amount see Color Key on pages 127); Worsted-weight or plastic canvas yarn (for amounts see Color Key).

CUTTING INSTRUCTIONS: Graphs and diagrams on pages 127–130.
NOTES: Use white canvas for N, S and T pieces.
A: For front and back, cut one each according to graphs.
B: For gabled and square sides, cut one according to graph and one 23 x 24 holes.
C: For bottom, cut one according to graph.
D: For bay window front, cut one 10 x 13 holes.
E: For bay window sides, cut two 4 x 13 holes (no graph).
F: For bay window top and bottom, cut one each according to graph.
G: For entry front, cut one according to graph.
H: For entry sides, cut two 5 x 8 holes.
I: For mat, cut one from 3" circle according to graph.
J: For entry roof, cut two 7 x 10 holes and two 4 x 7 holes (no graphs).

K: For shutters, cut four according to graph.
L: For hearts, cut two according to graph.
M: For balcony floor, cut one 5 x 11 holes.
N: For balcony rails, cut one front and two side pieces according to graphs.
O: For tall roof notched and square sides, cut one according to graph and one 28 x 29 holes.
P: For short roof, cut two according to graph.
Q: For roof facings, cut two tall and one short according to graphs.
R: For chimney sides, cut two according to graph and two 7 x 11 holes (no graph).
S: For roof rails, cut one long and two short according to graphs.
T: For window lattice, cut two according to graph.

STITCHING INSTRUCTIONS:

NOTE: S and T pieces are unworked.

1: Using colors and stitches indicated, work A-D (leave uncoded area of C unworked), G, I, K (two on opposite side of canvas), M, N (work one side rail substituting green for dk. orange and yellow for red), O and P (one on opposite side of canvas) pieces according to graphs. Fill in uncoded areas of A, B (leave indicated areas of front and gabled side unworked) and G pieces and work E, F, H and R pieces using rust and Continental Stitch. Using white and Continental Stitch, work J and short Q pieces.

2: With pink for hearts, dk. orange for curved edge of mat and with matching colors, Overcast unfinished edges of I, L, N (worked areas only) and Q pieces.

NOTE: Separate 1 yd. each of lime and green into 2-ply or nylon plastic canvas yarn into 1-ply.

3: Using 2-ply (or 1-ply) colors indicated, Straight Stitch and Lazy Daisy Stitch, embroider stems and leaves on

shutters and grass on entry sides and front as indicated on graphs. Using lime for motifs above side and front windows and door, variegated red/white for trim on doors, bay window and square side window and Straight Stitch, embroider as indicated. Using pink for dot trim under front, gabled side and entry front eaves and red for flowers on shutters and French Knot, embroider as indicated.

4: For bay window, with white, Whipstitch D-F pieces together according to Bay Window Assembly Diagram; Overcast unfinished edges. For entry, with white, Whipstitch G and H pieces together at matching bottom edges; Overcast unfinished top edges. For entry roof, holding long J pieces wrong sides together, with one strand each of red and pink, Whipstitch together at one matching short edge. With white, Whipstitch one short J to each long J according to Entry Roof Assembly Diagram; Overcast unfinished edges.

5: For front windows, with white, Overcast unfinished top and bottom edges of cutouts on front A. Holding wrong side of each K to right side of front, with lime, Whipstitch shutters to window edges as indicated; Overcast unfinished edges of shutters. For balcony, matching bottom edges of N pieces to M, with white, Whipstitch rails and floor together.

6: For tall roof, holding O pieces wrong sides together, with one strand each of red and pink, Whipstitch together at matching short, straight edges. For short roof, holding P pieces wrong sides together, Whipstitch together at matching long, straight edges. With white, Overcast unfinished edges of each roof.

7: For chimney, holding R pieces wrong sides together, alternating notched and straight sides and matching top edges, with white, Whipstitch together; Overcast unfinished bottom edges. With one strand each of red and

pink, Overcast top edges of chimney. Sew pre-gathered lace around top edge as shown.

NOTE: Cut four 6" lengths of pink.

8: For star trim, knot one end of each 6" strand of pink. For entry and balcony door trims, thread one 6" strand through center of one 12-mm. white bead, then through indicated hole; knot on wrong side of work. For gabled and square side trims, thread one 6" strand through center of one 12-mm. red star bead, through center of one 20-mm. white star bead, through center of white 18-mm. star bead, then through indicated hole; knot on wrong side.

NOTES: Cut one 5", one $\frac{3}{8}$" (one motif) and two $3\frac{1}{2}$" lengths of sculpted lace. Cut two $1\frac{1}{4}$" lengths of edging lace.

9: Sew twelve silver 3-mm. round beads to bay window and remaining silver beads to square side window as indicated. Sew one $1\frac{1}{4}$" length of edging lace to top edge of each window. Sew $5\frac{1}{2}$" and $\frac{3}{8}$" lengths of sculpted lace to bottom edge of front on either side of unworked area; sew one 4-mm. faceted bead to each motif. Sew one $3\frac{1}{2}$" length of sculpted to each side as above. Sew two lace motifs above each front window as shown in photo.

10: Matching bottom edges, with white, Whipstitch side edges of entry and balcony floor to front at indicated areas. Holding entry behind worked area of bottom, with white, Whipstitch front, back, sides and bottom together; Overcast unfinished edges.

11: Glue bay window over unworked area of gabled side and entry roof to entry and front. Glue corner edges of balcony rails together and side edges of rails to front. Glue one heart above each front window and T pieces behind each window as shown. Glue mat to bottom porch as shown. For roof rails, glue one 4-mm. faceted bead to each spike on each S piece.

12: Glue roof facings and roof pieces together as shown in House Roof Assembly Diagram. Glue roof rails and chimney to roofs as shown. Shape chenille stem and cover with fiberfill to form smoke trail; glue one end to inside of chimney. For tree, glue remaining green beads together; glue tree to one corner of house as shown. If desired, glue crystal glitter on roofs.

COLOR KEY: Gingerbread House

	4-ply or worsted-weight yarn			AMOUNT
■	Red/White Variegated			4 yds.

	Worsted-weight	Nylon Plus™	Need-loft™	YARN AMOUNT
■	White	#01	#41	2½ oz.
■	Rust	#51	#09	2 oz.
■	Pink	#11	#07	10 yds.
■	Red	#19	#02	8 yds.
■	Lime	#29	#22	7 yds.
■	Lt. Blue	#05	#36	4 yds.
■	Cinnamon	#44	#14	3 yds.
■	Green	#58	#28	2 yds.
■	Dk. Orange	#18	#52	1½ yds.
■	Tangerine	#15	#11	1 yd.
■	Yellow	#26	#57	1 yd.

STITCH KEY:

- — Backstitch/Straight Stitch
- ● French Knot
- ⬭ Lazy Daisy Stitch
- ☐ Unworked Area/Entry Attachment
- ☐ Unworked Area/Balcony Attachment
- ☐ Unworked Area/Bay Window Placement
- ○ Silver Bead Attachment
- ◆ Star Trim Attachment

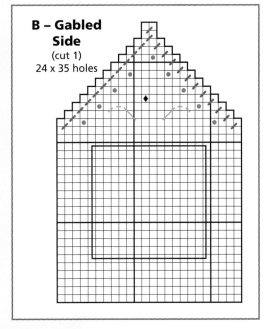

B – Gabled Side
(cut 1)
24 x 35 holes

B – Square Side
(cut 1)
23 x 24 holes

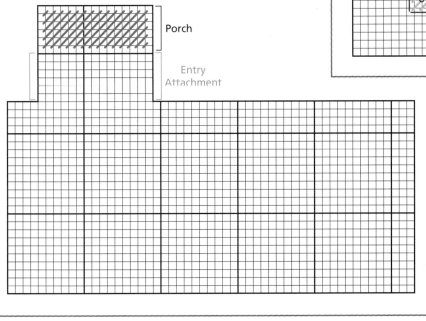

C – Bottom
(cut 1 each)
36 x 53 holes

Porch

Entry Attachment

G – Entry Front
(cut 1)
15 x 16 holes

**D – Bay
Window Front**
(cut 1) 10 x 13 holes

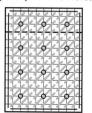

**Bay Window
Assembly
Diagram**

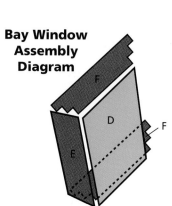

**Entry Roof
Assembly
Diagram**

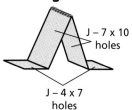

J – 7 x 10
holes

J – 4 x 7
holes

L – Heart
(cut 2)
2 x 2 holes

**F – Bay
Window Top
& Bottom**
(cut 1 each)
3 x 14 holes

I – Mat
(cut 1 from 3" circle)
1"

**N – Balcony
Side Rail**
(cut 2 from white)
4 x 5 holes

Cut out gray area carefully.

**N – Balcony
Front Rail**
(cut 1 from white)
4 x 11 holes

Cut out gray areas carefully.

M – Balcony Floor
(cut 1)
5 x 11 holes

Do not Overcast;
Whipstitch to front.

**H – Entry
Side**
(cut 2)
5 x 8 holes

A – Front
(cut 1)
45 x 53 holes

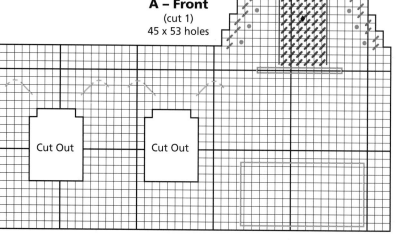

Cut Out   Cut Out

K – Shutters
(cut 4)
3 x 9 holes

Whipstitch to
front window.

COLOR KEY: Gingerbread House

4-ply or worsted-weight yarn	AMOUNT
Red/White Variegated	4 yds.

Worsted-weight	Nylon Plus™	Need-loft™	YARN AMOUNT
White	#01	#41	2½ oz.
Rust	#51	#09	2 oz.
Pink	#11	#07	10 yds.
Red	#19	#02	8 yds.
Lime	#29	#22	7 yds.
Lt. Blue	#05	#36	4 yds.
Cinnamon	#44	#14	3 yds.
Green	#58	#28	2 yds.
Dk. Orange	#18	#52	1½ yds.
Tangerine	#15	#11	1 yd.
Yellow	#26	#57	1 yd.

STITCH KEY:

- Backstitch/Straight Stitch
- French Knot
- Lazy Daisy Stitch
- Unworked Area/Entry Attachment
- Unworked Area/Balcony Attachment
- Unworked Area/Bay Window Placement
- O Silver Bead Attachment
- ◆ Star Trim Attachment

O – Tall Roof Notched Side
(cut 1) 28 x 29 holes

Whipstitch

Continue established pattern for square O.

P – Short Roof Side
(cut 2) 22 x 38 holes

Whipstitch

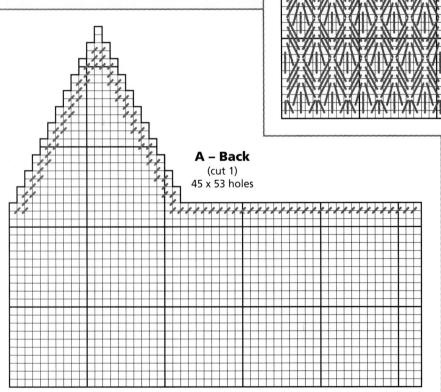

A – Back
(cut 1)
45 x 53 holes

House Roof Assembly Diagram

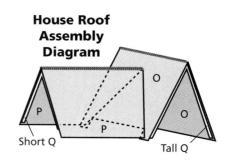

P

O

P

O

Short Q

Tall Q

S – Short Roof Rail
(cut 2) 3 x 14 holes

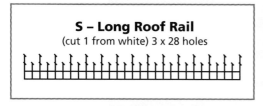

S – Long Roof Rail
(cut 1 from white) 3 x 28 holes

Q – Short Roof Facing
(cut 1) 18 x 18 holes

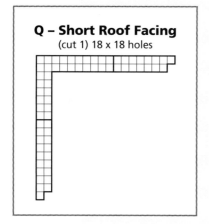

COLOR KEY: Gingerbread House

4-ply or worsted-weight yarn			AMOUNT
Red/White Variegated			4 yds.

Worsted-weight	Nylon Plus™	Need-loft™	YARN AMOUNT
White	#01	#41	2½ oz.
Rust	#51	#09	2 oz.
Pink	#11	#07	10 yds.
Red	#19	#02	8 yds.
Lime	#29	#22	7 yds.
Lt. Blue	#05	#36	4 yds.
Cinnamon	#44	#14	3 yds.
Green	#58	#28	2 yds.
Dk. Orange	#18	#52	1½ yds.
Tangerine	#15	#11	1 yd.
Yellow	#26	#57	1 yd.

STITCH KEY:
— Backstitch/Straight Stitch
● French Knot
⬯ Lazy Daisy Stitch
☐ Unworked Area/Entry Attachment
☐ Unworked Area/Balcony Attachment
☐ Unworked Area/Bay Window Placement
O Silver Bead Attachment
◆ Star Trim Attachment

R – Chimney Side
(cut 2)
8 x 10 holes

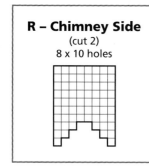

T – Window Lattice
(cut 2 from white)
16 x 16 holes

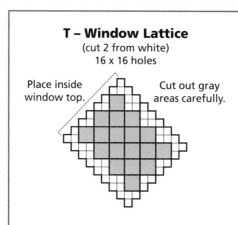

Place inside window top.

Cut out gray areas carefully.

Q – Tall Roof Facing
(cut 2)
21 x 22 holes

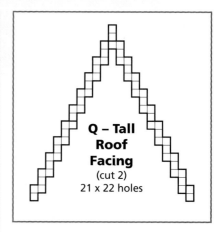

Hang this joyful banner on a festive holiday wreath to proclaim the joy of the season. Without the wreath, the stitched piece makes a beautiful accent for a mantel.

By Kathleen Hurley

Angelic Herald

131

Instructions begin next page

SIZE: 7⅜" x 17⅜".

MATERIALS: One sheet of 12" x 18" or larger 7-count plastic canvas; One 22" x 28" sheet of white poster board; Two 2" sawtooth hangers (optional); Craft glue or glue gun; Metallic cord (for amount see Color Key); Worsted-weight or plastic canvas yarn (for amounts see Color Key).

CUTTING INSTRUCTIONS:
A: For banner, cut one according to graph.
B: For backing, using A as a pat-

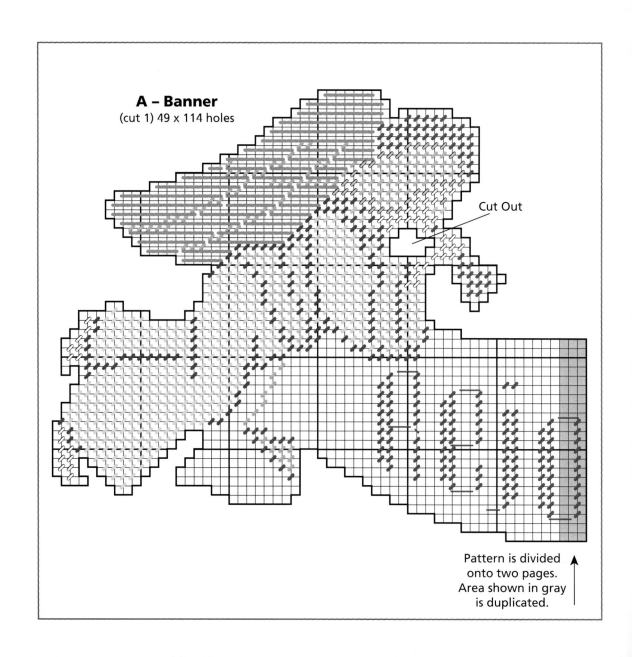

A – Banner
(cut 1) 49 x 114 holes

Cut Out

Pattern is divided onto two pages. Area shown in gray is duplicated.

tern, cut one from poster board ⅛" smaller at all edges.

STITCHING INSTRUCTIONS:

1: Using colors and stitches indicated, work A according to graph. Fill in uncoded areas using white and Continental Stitch. Using dk. red and Straight Stitch, embroider letter detail as indicated on graph. With lt. yellow for wings, dk. royal for gowns, dk. red for sleeves and collar, gold cord for white edges of banner and with matching colors, Overcast unfinished edges.

2: Glue backing and hangers to wrong side.

COLOR KEY: Angelic Herald

	Metallic cord			AMOUNT
■	Gold			10 yds.

	Worsted-weight	Nylon Plus™	Need-loft™	YARN AMOUNT
	White	#01	#41	24 yds.
	Dk. Red	#20	#01	14 yds.
	Sail Blue	#04	#35	14 yds.
	Dk. Royal	#07	#48	8 yds.
	Lt. Yellow	#42	#21	8 yds.
	Lt. Pink	#10	#08	6 yds.
	Pink	#11	#07	5 yds.
	Cinnamon	#44	#14	3 yds.
	Sand	#47	#16	2 yds.

STITCH KEY:

— Backstitch/Straight Stitch

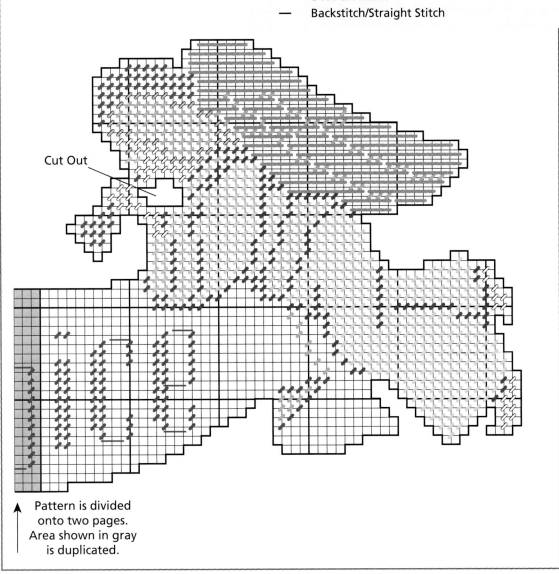

Cut Out

▲ Pattern is divided onto two pages. Area shown in gray is duplicated.

CELEBRATION GIFTS

By Trudy Bath Smith

Winter Sparkle

Capture the delicate beauty of a magical morning, when everything glitters with a frosting of new snow and a sprinkling of silvery ice crystals.

CELEBRATION GIFTS

CANDY BOWL
SIZE: 5½" x 5½" x 3½" tall.

MATERIALS: One sheet each of clear and white 7-count plastic canvas; Metallic cord (for amounts see Color Key on page 136); Worsted-weight or plastic canvas yarn (for amounts see Color Key).

CUTTING INSTRUCTIONS:
  A: For sides and side linings, cut four from each color according to graph on page 136.
  B: For bottom and bottom lining, cut two from white 11 x 11 holes (no graph).

STITCHING INSTRUCTIONS:

NOTE: White lining A pieces and B pieces are unworked.

1: Using colors and stitches indicated, work clear A pieces according to graph. Holding lining A pieces to wrong side of worked pieces, with white and working through all thicknesses, Whipstitch together as indicated on graph.

2: Holding B pieces together as one, Whipstitch sides and bottom together. With white/silver, Whipstitch unfinished edges of bowl together.

BASKET
SIZE: 7¾" x 7¾" x 9½" tall.

MATERIALS: Two sheets each of clear and white 7-count plastic canvas; Metallic cord (for amounts see Color Key on page 137); Worsted-weight or plastic canvas yarn (for amounts see Color Key).

CUTTING INSTRUCTIONS: Graphs on page 137.
  A: For sides, cut four from each color according to graph.
  B: For handle, cut one from each color according to graph.
  C: For bottom, cut two from white 15 x 15 holes (no graph).

according to graph.
B: For Box sides, cut seven from each color 8 x 11 holes.
C: For Box bottom, cut one from each color according to graph.

STITCHING INSTRUCTIONS:

NOTE: White A and B and both C pieces are unworked.

1: Using colors and stitches indicated, work A and B pieces according to graphs. For each Coaster, holding one unworked A to wrong side of worked piece, with white/silver, Whipstitch together.

2: To join Box sides, holding unworked B pieces to wrong side of worked pieces and working through all thicknesses, with white, Whipstitch together, leaving final two pieces unjoined.

NOTE: For lining pieces, using assembled side and one C as a pattern, cut one each from felt ⅛" smaller at all edges.

3: For Box, holding C pieces together as one with clear piece facing inside, Whipstitch sides and bottom together (see photo). With white/silver, Whipstitch unfinished edges together. Glue lining pieces inside box as shown.

WREATH
SIZE: 10" across x 13" high.

MATERIALS: ½ sheet of 7-count plastic canvas; Three 9" plastic canvas circles; Two white 3" Crafty Circles; Two blue 11-mm. round acrylic stones; 1½ yds. silver ¼" picot-edged ribbon; Silver rose leaves; White floral tape; Metal coat hanger; Wire cutters; Craft glue or glue gun; Metallic cord (for amount see Color Key on page 138);

STITCHING INSTRUCTIONS:

NOTE: White lining A pieces and C pieces are unworked.

1: Using colors and stitches indicated, work clear A and B pieces according to graphs. Holding lining A pieces to wrong side of worked pieces, with white and working through all thicknesses, Whipstitch together as indicated on graph. Holding lining B to wrong side of worked piece, with white/silver, Whipstitch together.

2: Holding C pieces together as one, with white, Whipstitch A and C pieces together. With white/silver, Whipstitch unfinished edges of basket together, catching ends of handle on opposite sides to join as shown in photo.

COASTERS & BOX
SIZE: Each Coaster is 3⅞" x 3⅞"; Box is 4⅜" across x 1⅜" tall.

MATERIALS: One sheet each of clear and white 7-count plastic canvas; Scrap of white felt; Craft glue or glue gun; Metallic cord (for amount see Color Key on page 138); Worsted-weight or plastic canvas yarn (for amounts see Color Key).

CUTTING INSTRUCTIONS: Graphs on page 138.
A: For Coasters, cut four from each color

COLOR KEY: Candy Bowl

Metallic cord			AMOUNT
☐ White/Silver			3 yds.

Worsted-weight	Nylon Plus™	Need-loft™	YARN AMOUNT
White	#01	#41	12 yds.
Sail Blue	#04	#35	7 yds.
Lt. Blue	#05	#36	5 yds.

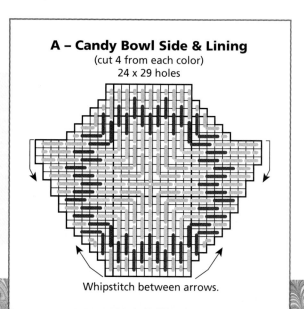

A – Candy Bowl Side & Lining
(cut 4 from each color)
24 x 29 holes

Whipstitch between arrows.

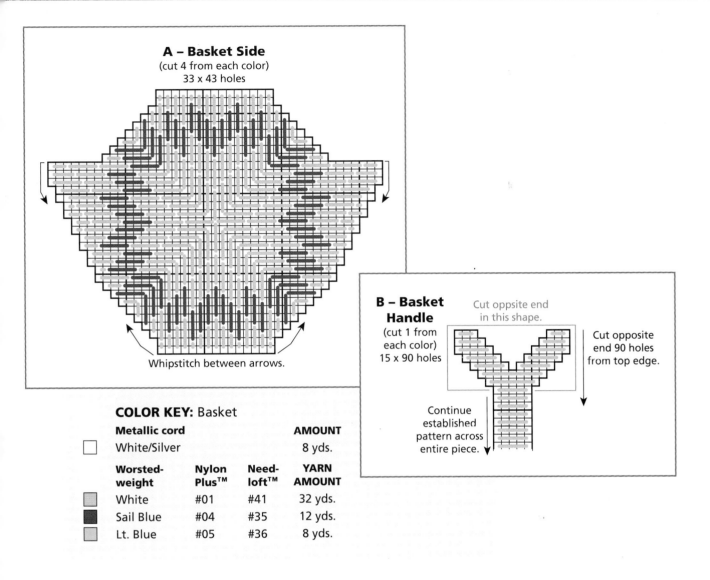

A – Basket Side
(cut 4 from each color)
33 x 43 holes

Whipstitch between arrows.

B – Basket Handle
(cut 1 from each color)
15 x 90 holes

Cut oppsite end in this shape.

Cut opposite end 90 holes from top edge.

Continue established pattern across entire piece.

COLOR KEY: Basket

	Metallic cord			AMOUNT
☐	White/Silver			8 yds.

	Worsted-weight	Nylon Plus™	Need-loft™	YARN AMOUNT
☐	White	#01	#41	32 yds.
■	Sail Blue	#04	#35	12 yds.
☐	Lt. Blue	#05	#36	8 yds.

Worsted-weight or plastic canvas yarn (for amounts see Color Key).

CUTTING INSTRUCTIONS: Graphs and illustration on page 139.
A: For welcome sign, cut two according to graph.
B: For wreath pieces, cut one from each 9" circle according to graph; cut through each piece as indicated.
C: For snowflakes, cut one from each Crafty Circle according to graph. (NOTE: Graph grid may not exactly match your canvas.)

STITCHING INSTRUCTIONS:

1: Using colors and stitches indicated, work one A and C pieces according to graph. For welcome sign, holding unworked A to wrong side of worked piece, with white/silver, Whipstitch together.

2: For wreath, using sail blue for two pieces and lt. blue for remaining piece, finish inner edge of each B according to Wreath Stitch Illustration. With white/silver, Overcast unfinished outer edge of each piece.

3: For snowflakes, with white/silver, Overcast unfinished inside and outside edges of outer circles.

ASSEMBLY:

1: Loosely braid B pieces together; with matching colors, Whipstitch ends together to close each circle. Wrap yarn several times around the three circles at the seam area, and glue to secure. Arrange leaves in clusters and wrap with floral tape to secure.

NOTE: Cut one 8" and two 3½" lengths of white/silver.

2: Thread each 3½" strand of white/silver through back upper corners of welcome sign; knot ends behind work. Thread opposite ends through yarn at bottom back of wreath; knot ends.

COLOR KEY: Wreath

Metallic cord			AMOUNT
☐ White/Silver			15 yds.

Worsted-weight	Nylon Plus™	Need-loft™	YARN AMOUNT
■ Sail Blue	#04	#35	19 yds.
☐ Lt. Blue	#05	#36	17 yds.

3: Thread 8" strand of white/silver through stitches at outer edge of one snowflake, hiding yarn end behind stitches. Thread opposite end through yarn at top of wreath, then through stitches at outer edge of remaining snowflake. Glue ends to secure. Balance snowflakes on cord as desired; glue together at one point to hold.

NOTE: Cut coat hanger wire to 27" length.

4: Bend wire into a circle; bend ends back over each other to hold; wrap ends with floral tape. Holding hanger behind wreath with joint at top, wrap ribbon in and around both wreath and hanger to join.

5: With ribbon, make two double-loop bows; tie together. Trim two ends short, and leave remaining ends about 6" long. Glue bow to top of wreath. Glue long ribbon ends, curled decoratively, on either side of wreath as shown in photo. Glue stones to snowflake centers and leaf clusters to bottom of wreath as shown. ⌐

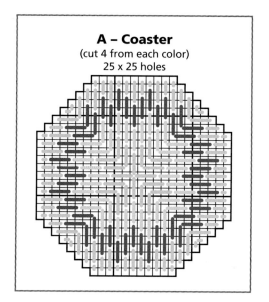

A – Coaster
(cut 4 from each color)
25 x 25 holes

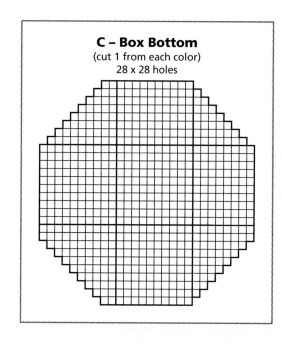

C – Box Bottom
(cut 1 from each color)
28 x 28 holes

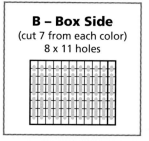

B – Box Side
(cut 7 from each color)
8 x 11 holes

COLOR KEY: Coasters

Metallic cord			AMOUNT
☐ White/Silver			8 yds.

Worsted-weight	Nylon Plus™	Need-loft™	YARN AMOUNT
☐ White	#01	#41	17 yds.
■ Sail Blue	#04	#35	7 yds.
☐ Lt. Blue	#05	#36	6 yds.

B – Wreath Piece
(cut 1 from each 9" circle)

Cut away
gray center.

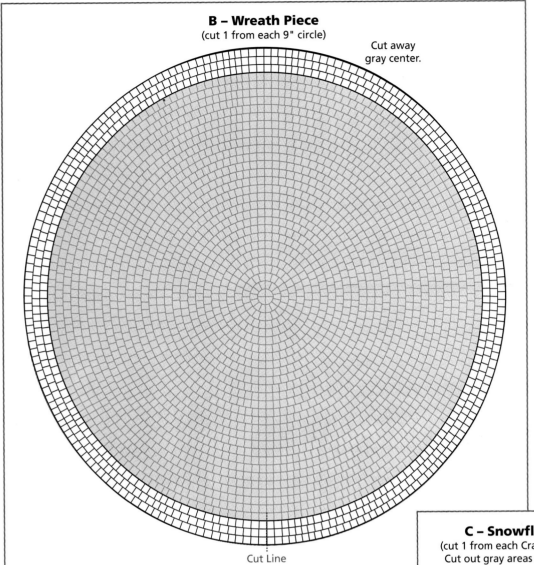

Cut Line

C – Snowflake
(cut 1 from each Crafty Circle)
Cut out gray areas carefully.

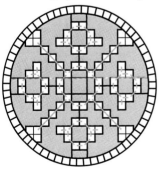

A – Welcome Sign
(cut 2) 13 x 51 holes

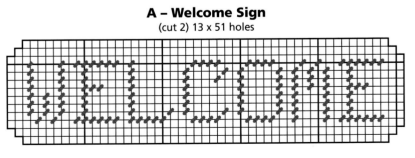

**Wreath Stitch
Illustration**

CELEBRATION GIFTS

By Michele Wilcox

Victorian Sleigh

**Lovely atop a piano or mantelpiece,
this charming, old-fashioned
Victorian folk-art sleigh will hold
goodies, greenery or greeting cards.**

CELEBRATION GIFTS

SIZE: 4" x 6⅛" x 10" long.

MATERIALS: 1½ sheets of 7-count plastic canvas; Craft glue or glue gun; Worsted-weight or plastic canvas yarn (for amounts see Color Key).

CUTTING INSTRUCTIONS:
A: For sides, cut two according to graph.
B: For front, cut one 17 x 23 holes (no graph).
C: For back, cut one 21 x 23 holes (no graph).
D: For bottom, cut one 23 x 25 holes (no graph).

STITCHING INSTRUCTIONS:

1: Using colors indicated and Continental Stitch, work A pieces on opposite sides of canvas according to graph. Fill in uncoded areas using pink and Continental Stitch; Overcast unfinished edges. Using colors and stitches indicated, work B-D pieces according to Sleigh Stitch Pattern Guide.

2: With mint, Whipstitch and assemble pieces according to Sleigh Assembly Diagram. ⬭

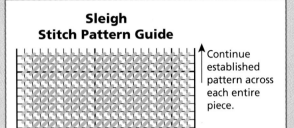

Sleigh Stitch Pattern Guide

Continue established pattern across each entire piece.

COLOR KEY: Victorian Sleigh

Worsted-weight	Nylon Plus™	Need-loft™	YARN AMOUNT
Pink	#11	#07	42 yds.
Mint	#30	#24	32 yds.
White	#01	#41	3 yds.

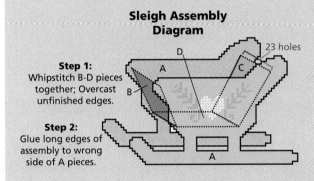

Sleigh Assembly Diagram

Step 1: Whipstitch B-D pieces together; Overcast unfinished edges.

Step 2: Glue long edges of assembly to wrong side of A pieces.

23 holes

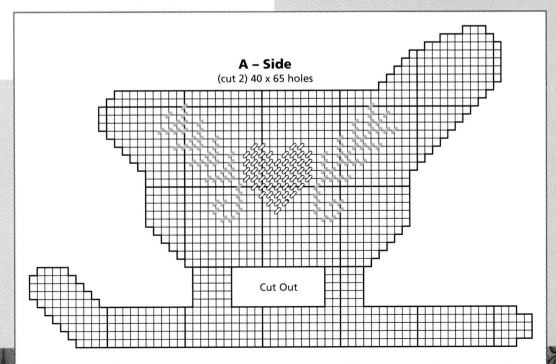

A – Side
(cut 2) 40 x 65 holes

Cut Out

QUICK GIFTS

CELEBRATION GIFTS

Little Things

BIRDHOUSE
By Lilo Fruehwirth

SIZE: 1⅞" x 2⅝" x 2" tall.

MATERIALS FOR ONE: Scraps of 7-count plastic canvas; One toothpick; 12" gold six-strand embroidery floss (for hanger) or one bamboo skewer (for plant poke); 10" blue ⅛" satin ribbon; Black craft paint; Spanish moss; Craft glue or glue gun; Six-strand embroidery floss (for amounts see Color Key); Worsted-weight or plastic canvas yarn (for amounts see Color Key).

CUTTING INSTRUCTIONS:
A: For front, cut one according to graph.
B: For sides and back, cut three 9 x 9 holes.
C: For roof, cut two 12 x 12 holes.

STITCHING INSTRUCTIONS:

NOTE: C piece is unworked.

1: Using white for house front, sides and back and sail blue for roof pieces and Continental Stitch, work A-C pieces. With white, Overcast unfinished cutout edges of A.

2: Using six strands floss in colors indicated, Straight Stitch and Lazy Daisy Stitch, embroider details as indicated on graphs.

3: With white, Whipstitch A and B pieces together, forming house; Overcast unfinished edges. Holding C pieces wrong sides together, with sail blue, Whipstitch together at one matching edge, forming roof; Overcast unfinished edges.

NOTE: Snap one end off toothpick; discard short end. Paint with black craft paint; let dry.

4: Insert pointed end of toothpick into house below cutout as indicated; glue to secure. Glue roof to house as shown in photo. For hanger, run gold floss through top center of roof; knot at roofline, and tie ends together. For plant poke, place one end of skewer inside bottom center of house; glue to secure.

HEART FRIDGIES
By Vicki Watkins

SIZE: 2½" x 3".

MATERIALS FOR ONE OF EACH: Scraps of 7-count plastic canvas; Three 2" magnetic strips; Craft glue or glue gun; Worsted-weight or plastic canvas yarn (for amounts see Color Key on page 146).

COLOR KEY: Birdhouse

Embroidery floss			AMOUNT
Green			6 yds.
Red			4 yds.
Pink			2½ yds.

Worsted-weight	Nylon Plus™	Need-loft™	YARN AMOUNT
White	#01	#41	9 yds.
Sail Blue	#04	#35	7 yds.

STITCH KEY:
— Backstitch/Straight Stitch
⌒ Lazy Daisy Stitch
◆ Toothpick Placement

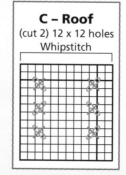

A – Front
(cut 1) 9 x 9 holes
Roof Center / Cut Out

C – Roof
(cut 2) 12 x 12 holes
Whipstitch

B – Side/Back
(cut 3) 9 x 9 holes

CELEBRATION GIFTS

Precious bird houses are delightful as
hanging ornaments or plant pokes.
Sweetheart designs make cute fridgies,
pins, package trims and more.

CUTTING INSTRUCTIONS:
   A: For each fridgie, cut one according to graph.

STITCHING INSTRUCTIONS:

1: Using colors and stitches indicated, work A pieces according to graphs. Fill in uncoded areas using white and Continental Stitch (slant stitches in direction of motifs). With red, Overcast unfinished edges.

2: Using black and Backstitch, embroider shirt detail according to graph. Glue magnetic strips to backs.

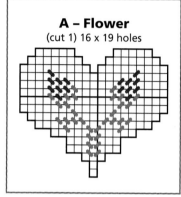

A – Flower
(cut 1) 16 x 19 holes

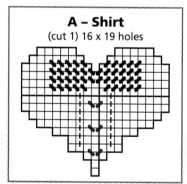

A – Shirt
(cut 1) 16 x 19 holes

COLOR KEY: Heart Fridgies

Worsted-weight		Nylon Plus™	Need-loft™	YARN AMOUNT
	White	#01	#41	9 yds.
	Red	#19	#02	5 yds.
	Black	#02	#00	2½ yds.
	Forest	#32	#29	2 yds.

STITCH KEY:
— Backstitch/Straight Stitch

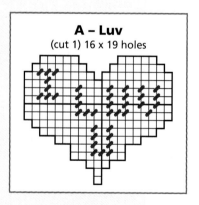

A – Luv
(cut 1) 16 x 19 holes

CELEBRATION GIFTS

By Fran Rohus

Trinkets & Treasures

Lavande

BOTANICS-SEHEN

BOTANICUS
Savon végétal

Good things come in small — and wonderful — packages with these tiny containers. They're just right for giving a gift to a special teacher or friend.

Patterns begin next page.

IRIS BOX
SIZE: 4" x 4¼" x 1⅝" tall.

MATERIALS: ½ sheet of 7-count plastic canvas; Worsted-weight or plastic canvas yarn (for amounts see Color Key).

CUTTING INSTRUCTIONS:
A: For lid top, cut one 25 x 28 holes.
B: For lid sides, cut two 3 x 25 holes and two 3 x 28 holes (no graphs).
C: For box bottom, cut one 23 x 27 holes (no graph).
D: For box sides, cut two 9 x 23 holes and two 9 x 27 holes (no graphs).

COLOR KEY: Iris Box

Worsted-weight	Nylon Plus™	Need-loft™	YARN AMOUNT
■ Lavender	#22	#45	25 yds.
▨ Aqua	#60	#51	15 yds.
☐ Straw	#41	#19	10 yds.

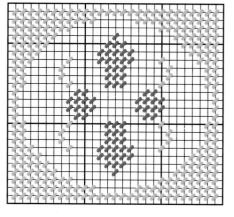

A – Iris Box Lid Top
(cut 1) 25 x 28 holes

**Iris Box Side
Stitch Pattern Guide**

Continue established pattern
across each entire piece.

STITCHING INSTRUCTIONS:

NOTE: C piece is unworked.

1: Using colors indicated and Continental Stitch, work A according to graph. Fill in uncoded areas using straw and Continental Stitch. Using lavender and Slanted Gobelin Stitch over narrow width, work B pieces. Using lavender and stitches indicated, work D pieces according to Iris Box Side Stitch Pattern Guide.

2: With aqua, Whipstitch A and B pieces together, forming lid; Whipstitch C and D pieces together, forming box. Overcast unfinished edges of lid and box.

DAINTY GIFT BAG
SIZE: 1⅞" x 2¾" x 3⅛" tall, not including handles.

MATERIALS: ½ sheet of 7-count plastic canvas; Velcro® closure; Craft glue or glue gun; Worsted-weight or plastic canvas yarn (for amounts see Color Key).

CUTTING INSTRUCTIONS:
A: For side, cut one 20 x 52 holes.
B: For bottom, cut one according to graph.
C: For handles, cut two 2 x 24 holes (no graph).
D: For flap, cut one 5 x 16 holes.

STITCHING INSTRUCTIONS:

1: Using straw and Continental Stitch, work A (overlap three holes at short ends as indicated on graph and work through both thicknesses at overlap area to join), B, C and D pieces. Using green and Lazy Daisy Stitch for leaves and purple and French Knot for flowers, embroider A and D pieces as indicated on graphs.

2: With straw and easing to fit, Whipstitch A and B pieces together, forming bag. Overcast unfinished edges of bag, flap and handles. Tack one short end of D to one side of A centered five holes from top edge. Tack handle ends to top edge of bag as shown in photo.

3: For closure, glue closure to inside of untacked end of flap and corresponding area on bag side.

B – Dainty Gift Bag Bottom
(cut 1) 12 x 18 holes

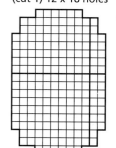

D – Dainty Gift Bag Flap
(cut 1) 5 x 16 holes

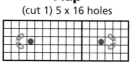

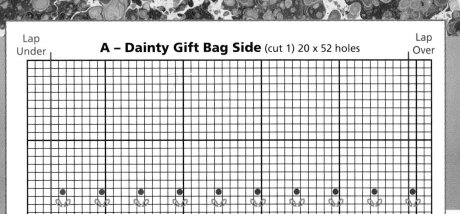

A – Dainty Gift Bag Side (cut 1) 20 x 52 holes

Lap Under

Lap Over

COLOR KEY: Dainty Gift Bag

Worsted-weight	Nylon Plus™	Need-loft™	YARN AMOUNT
Straw	#41	#19	30 yds.
Green	#58	#28	2 yds.
Purple	#21	#46	1½ yds.

STITCH KEY:

- ● French Knot
- ◡ Lazy Daisy Stitch

CELEBRATION GIFTS

From the Heart

Heart Plant Poke pattern on page 152.

Stitch this sweetheart plant poke or tissue cover in a flash to give to a new Mom, a shut-in or anyone who needs a gift of love.

CELEBRATION GIFTS

HEART TISSUE COVER
By Kristine Hart

SIZE: Loosely covers a boutique-style tissue box.

MATERIALS: 1½ sheets of 7-count plastic canvas; Velcro® closure (optional) Worsted-weight or plastic canvas yarn (for amounts see Color Key).

CUTTING INSTRUCTIONS:
    A: For sides, cut four 32 x 36 holes.
    B: For top, cut one according to graph.
    C: For optional bottom, cut one 32 x 32 holes and one 12 x 32 holes (no graphs).

STITCHING INSTRUCTIONS:

NOTE: C pieces are unworked.

1: Using colors and stitches indicated, work A and B pieces according to graphs.

2: With white, Overcast cutout edges of B. Whipstitch A and B pieces together, forming cover.

3: For optional cover bottom, Whipstitch unworked C pieces together at one matching edge according to Optional Bottom Assembly Diagram. Whipstitch opposite edge of bottom to one side of cover; Overcast unfinished edges. If desired, glue closure to flap and inside of cover.⌁

COLOR KEY: Tissue Cover

	Worsted-weight	Nylon Plus™	Need-loft™	YARN AMOUNT
	White	#01	#41	25 yds.
	Sail Blue	#04	#35	15 yds.
	Pink	#11	#07	12 yds.
	Sea Green	#37	#53	10 yds.

Optional Cover Bottom Assembly Diagram

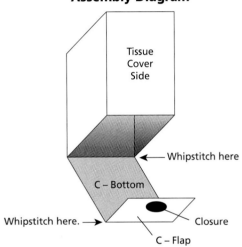

Tissue Cover Side

Whipstitch here

C – Bottom

Whipstitch here. →

Closure

C – Flap

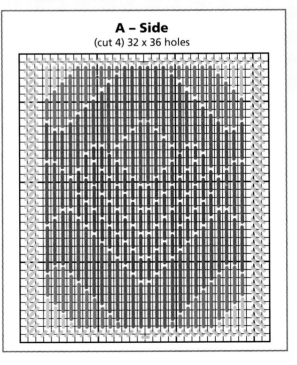

A – Side
(cut 4) 32 x 36 holes

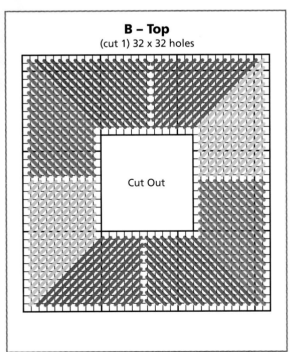

B – Top
(cut 1) 32 x 32 holes

Cut Out

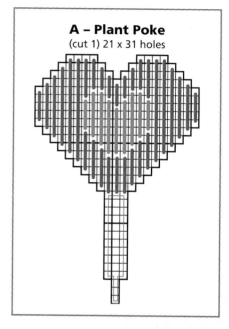

A – Plant Poke
(cut 1) 21 x 31 holes

HEART PLANT POKE

By Jocelyn Sass

SIZE: 3¼" x 4¾" tall.

MATERIALS: Scraps of 7-count plastic canvas; Worsted-weight or plastic canvas yarn (for amounts see Color Key).

CUTTING INSTRUCTIONS:

A: For Plant Poke, cut one according to graph.

STITCHING INSTRUCTIONS:

1: Using colors and stitches indicated, work A according to graph, leaving indicated area unworked. With white, Overcast unfinished edges of worked area. ⬭

COLOR KEY: Plant Poke

	Worsted-weight	Nylon Plus™	Need-loft™	YARN AMOUNT
■	Pink	#11	#07	2 yds.
▦	White	#01	#41	2 yds.

STITCH KEY:

☐ Unworked area

CELEBRATION GIFTS

Card Party

For the card player on your gift list, this set of accessories will inspire a fun get-together. Include a new deck of cards with the card box, score pad holder and snack picks.

153

Patterns begin next page.

SIZE: Card Box is 4³⁄₈" x 6¹⁄₈" x 1³⁄₄" tall; Note Pad Cover is 3" x 5"; Snack Picks are 1" x 1".

MATERIALS FOR ONE OF EACH: One sheet of 7-count plastic canvas; Scraps of 10-count plastic canvas; 3" x 5" bottom-opening spiral notebook; Four toothpicks; Craft glue or glue gun; Worsted-weight or plastic canvas yarn (for amounts see Color Key).

CARD BOX
By Helen Miller

CUTTING INSTRUCTIONS:
   NOTE: Use 7-count canvas throughout.
   A: For lid top, cut one 28 x 40 holes.
   B: For lid sides, cut two 7 x 40 holes.
   C: For lid ends, cut two 7 x 28 holes (no graph).
   D: For box bottom, cut one 28 x 40 holes (no graph).
   E: For box sides, cut two 7 x 38 holes (no graph).
   F: For box ends, cut two 7 x 26 holes (no graph).
   G: For box divider, cut one 7 x 25 holes (no graph).

STITCHING INSTRUCTIONS:

NOTE: E-G pieces are unworked.

1: Using colors indicated and Continental Stitch, work A and B pieces according to graphs. Fill in uncoded areas and work C pieces using white and Continental Stitch. Using black and Continental Stitch, work D. Using black, Backstitch and Straight

Stitch, embroider letters on B as indicated on graph.

2: For box lid, with white, Whipstitch A-C pieces together; with red, Overcast unfinished edges.

3: For box, Whipstitch D-G pieces together according to Card Box Assembly Diagram. With red, Overcast unfinished edges of box.

NOTE PAD COVER
By Sandra Miller-Maxfield

CUTTING INSTRUCTIONS:
   Note: Use 7-count canvas.
   A: For pad cover, cut one 20 x 33 holes.

STITCHING INSTRUCTIONS:

1: Using red and Continental Stitch, work A according to graph. Fill in uncoded area using white and Continental Stitch.

NOTE: Separate 12" of black into 2-ply or nylon plastic canvas yarn into 1-ply strands.

2: Using 2-ply (or 1-ply) black and Straight Stitch, embroider letters as indicated on graph. With black, Overcast unfinished edges. Glue to notebook cover.

SNACK PICKS
By Sandra Miller-Maxfield

CUTTING INSTRUCTIONS:
   NOTE: Use 10-count canvas throughout.
   A: For diamond, cut one according to graph.
   B: For spade, cut one according to graph.
   C: For club, cut one according to graph.
   D: For heart, cut one according to graph.

STITCHING INSTRUCTIONS:

NOTE: Separate 2 yds. each black and red into 2-ply or nylon plastic canvas yarn into 1-ply strands; use separated yarn throughout.

1: Using red for heart and diamond and black for spade and club and Continental Stitch, work A-D pieces.

2: With matching colors, Overcast unfinished edges. Glue to toothpicks. ⌒

A – Card Box Lid Top
(cut 1) 28 x 40 holes

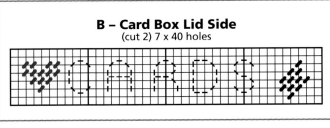

A – Note Pad Cover
(cut 1) 20 x 33 holes

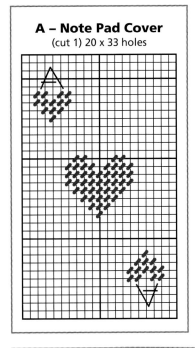

B – Card Box Lid Side
(cut 2) 7 x 40 holes

A – Snack Picks Diamond
(cut 1) 9 x 11 holes

Step 1:
With white,
Whipstitch E and F
pieces together.

**Card Box Assembly
Diagram**

Step 2:
With black, Whipstitch
E-F assembly to first
bar inside edge of D.

Step 3:
With white,
Whipstitch G to sides
and bottom.

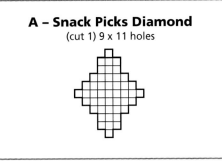

COLOR KEY: Card Party

	Worsted-weight	Nylon Plus™	Need-loft™	YARN AMOUNT
White		#01	#41	42 yds.
Black		#02	#00	32 yds.
Red		#19	#02	12 yds.

STITCH KEY:

— Backstitch/Straight Stitch

C – Snack Picks Club
(cut 1) 11 x 11 holes

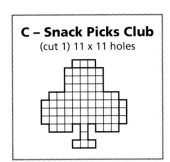

D – Snack Picks Heart
(cut 1) 10 x 11 holes

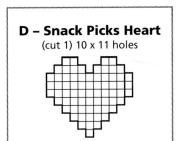

B – Snack Picks Spade
(cut 1) 10 x 12 holes

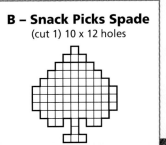

By Dorris Brooks

Orchid Angles

SIZE: 3" x 11¾" x 8⅞" tall, not including handles.

MATERIALS: Six sheets of 7-count plastic canvas; Monofilament fishing line; Worsted-weight or plastic canvas yarn (for amounts see Color Key on page 158).

CUTTING INSTRUCTIONS: Graphs and diagram on pages 158–159.
  A: For sides and linings, cut two 58 x 77 holes and two 56 x 75 holes (no lining graph).
  B: For ends and linings, cut two 19 x 58 holes and two 17 x 56 holes (no lining graph).
  C: For bottom and lining, cut one 19 x 77 holes and one 17 x 75 holes (no lining graph).
  D: For handles, cut two 5 x 80 holes (no graph).

STITCHING INSTRUCTIONS:

NOTE: Lining pieces are unworked.

1: Using colors and stitches indicated, work A-C pieces according to graphs. Using orchid and Slanted Gobelin Stitch over narrow width, work D pieces. With plum, Overcast unfinished long edges of handles.

2: Holding worked A-C pieces wrong sides together, with plum, Whipstitch together, forming bag; Overcast unfinished edges. Whipstitch lining pieces together; Overcast unfinished edges.

3: Place lining inside bag, and place ends of each handle three holes deep between lining and bag according to Tote Bag Assembly Diagram. With fishing line, sew lining, bag and handles together around top edge. ▱

Fresh colors and bold angles create this stunning, fashionable tote that's as much fun to make as it is to use. It's great for toting needlework in progress.

CELEBRATION GIFTS

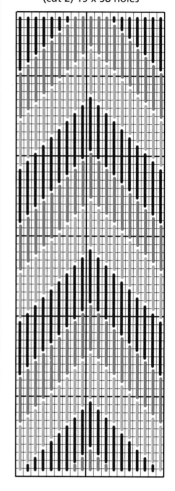

B – End
(cut 2) 19 x 58 holes

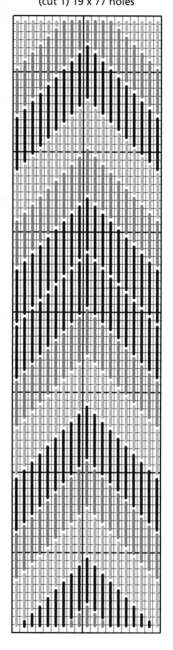

C – Bottom
(cut 1) 19 x 77 holes

COLOR KEY: Orchid Angles

Worsted-weight		Nylon Plus™	Need-loft™	YARN AMOUNT
☐	Orchid	#56	#44	3 oz.
■	Plum	#55	#59	3 oz.
▨	Silver	#40	#37	2¹⁄₂ oz.

A – Side (cut 2) 58 x 77 holes

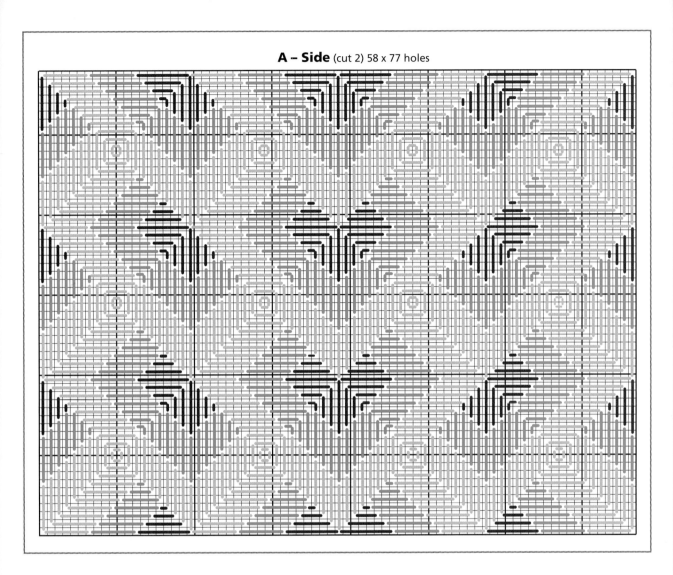

Tote Bag Assembly Diagram

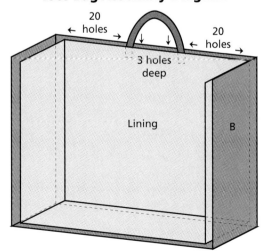

20 holes

20 holes

3 holes deep

Lining

B

CELEBRATION GIFTS

INDEX